La Conchita

La Conchita

A Different Kind of Paradise

Bonnie G. Kelm, Ph.D.

In memory of Maggie Haumann
Author, song writer, vocalist, surfer, duck wrangler, and Renaissance woman
Her light shines in the setting sun, dances on the ocean waves
and waits for us on the banks of many rivers

America Through Time is an imprint of Fonthill Media LLC
www.through-time.com
office@through-time.com

Published by Arcadia Publishing by arrangement with Fonthill Media LLC
For all general information, please contact Arcadia Publishing:
Telephone: 843-853-2070
Fax: 843-853-0044
E-mail: sales@arcadiapublishing.com
For customer service and orders:
Toll-Free 1-888-313-2665

www.arcadiapublishing.com

First published 2019

ISBN 978-1- 63499-181-0

Typeset in 10pt on 13pt Sabon
Printed and bound in England

Acknowledgments

First, I wish to extend my gratitude to Alan Sutton, President of Fonthill Media, for having faith in this book. Grateful appreciation is also expressed to Matthew Rodriguez, acquisitions editor at America Through Time, for inviting me to write this book, and Jamie Hardwick, project editor, Fonthill Media, for his endless patience with the unforeseen calamities that I seem to attract. Thanks also go to Kena Longabaugh for her graciousness under fire.

The seeds for first the book chapter, then the exhibition, and now the whole La Conchita story would not have even sprouted without those first tantalizing pieces of history offered to me by my original trio of resources; Jeff Ross, Eleanor Gallardo Ramey, and Chet Dacayana. In turn, they led me to Bill Mingus, Federico (Dick) Talaugon Jr., Allen and Ray Blackwell, Pete Richardson, and Robbie Hutto, who provided the oral histories and photo archives enabling me to begin to assemble the story of this unique community. It has been such an honor and a privilege to work with them all. Ten years ago, the success of the La Conchita exhibition was greatly enriched by the addition of significant new material from the collections of B. Talaugon Dunn and Mary Giles McDonough. This book would be significantly diminished without these materials.

Additional gratitude for vital photographic contributions go to Rob Malone; Yan Richardson; Janell Beck; Ben Dacayana; the Lindley Institute; Lisa Stone, curator of the Roger Brown Study Collection, School of the Art Institute of Chicago; Linda Merrill; the Oren Family Archive; the Alvis Family; and Rob Freeman. My eternal thanks go to all the resources that helped bring this book to fruition, kept me from stepping on too many toes and those saved me from totally losing my mind. Thank you; Penny Little Savage, David Griggs, Director, Carpinteria Valley Historical Museum, Kathy Klock, and Rob Malone. Last, but certainly not least, I wish to express my deepest appreciation to my husband Bill, who not only assisted in organizing my bibliographic files and went on my scavenger hunts for information with me. He also excelled at hand-holding.

CONTENTS

Preface

My adventure in writing this history of La Conchita really began not long after we moved here. Just three doors down and across the street from my house is the oldest house in La Conchita. The woman who introduced herself to me and told me all about it is now gone, but just thinking about her brings a smile to my face. I have always loved old houses, so on my way to the beach or the mailbox, I would stop and really look at this house every day. I could tell it had a lot to say. One day, a woman showed up next to me and told me that she has seen me looking at her house. I smiled and said that old houses can tell you a lot about the history of a place. That was when she told me about how her father built the house after he came here from Mexico with no money to work for the railroad in 1918. He was able to buy this property and build the first house in La Conchita nine years later. That was my introduction to Eleanor Gallardo Ramey.

She had many wonderful stories about La Conchita to share, and I enjoyed hearing all of them. She sheepishly told me that she was one of the eleven children her parents had in that house. We both laughed when she solemnly related that her family provided the entire Mexican population of La Conchita in the early years. I asked her lots of questions and was really amazed by what she was telling me because the general opinion about this area was that nothing good ever happened here. I am glad I was never one of those people who listened to hearsay. Three days later, Eleanor showed up at my doorstep with forty-eight old photos in an old shoebox and the rest is history.

Prior to my seven years of research, there was a dearth of factual information or any history about La Conchita's past in the files of the Ventura, Carpinteria, and Santa Barbara Historical Society libraries. Now, there is a significant archive of photos, documents, and oral histories from the "La Conchita Elders," who shared recollections with me going back to 1923. The "La Conchita Elders" is the name I gave to the first generation of people who grew up in La Conchita and still survived to tell their stories. The initial result of this research was written for Greater Carpinteria, Summerland, and La Conchita, which I jointly authored with Jim Campos, Dave Moore, and

Jim Moore, with the assistance of the Carpinteria Valley Historical Society in 2009. That was the first documented written history of La Conchita. I subsequently curated the exhibition "La Conchita: Reclaiming Its History" at the Carpinteria Valley Historical Society Museum. The exhibition not only gave me more space to share additional research and photos, but it also gave me a platform to collect further information about La Conchita's history. At the time of the exhibition (2010–2011), a number of the La Conchita Elders whose oral histories became the backbone of this story were still alive and able to attend the exhibition opening or got to see the exhibition during the year it was on view. It was really touching to have so many people who grew up in La Conchita show up for the opening of this exhibition. Many of them attended the Punta Gorda School and wanted to pay tribute to Robert Bates and especially Bessie Davison. A number of others joined me in La Conchita and held "conception parties." Most moving of all, and I must preserve their privacy, was the paddle out in the bay for the family who brought the ashes of their mother and father to be released in the bay. They told me the best days of their lives together as a family was spent in La Conchita.

Sadly, now ten years later, all of that first generation is gone. I feel very fortunate to have known each of them and to relate the remarkable story of how, against all odds, an unlikely group of people banded together and built a different kind of paradise on the Gold Coast of California. That story continues to shape the character of La Conchita to the present day. As I went through all of the oral histories I had collected, there were so many poignant stories about the life and times growing up in this unique community that I knew their stories had to be told in their own words. Except for my own observations, mostly at the end of the book, all of the photos, history, and commentary come directly from the first generations to grow up in La Conchita until 1959, when running water first came from Lake Casitas and La Conchita became a more populated community.

Opposite above: The author with Ben Dacayana at the opening of the La Conchita Exhibition, September 2010. (*Author's collection*)

Opposite below: Benny Dacayana and Paulie Talaugon, *c.* mid-1940s; the photo was displayed at the the 2010 La Conchita Exhibition. (*Ben Dacayana*)

1

Overview

> Wil rested his arm on the open window; to the left, La Conchita appealed to some inner sense. It was so unexpected: half mile long, scrunched against the coastal cliffs, a vest pocket colony not even on most road maps. Northbound drivers escaping L.A. for the red tiled splendors of Santa Barbara another fifteen minutes up the road rarely caught more than two blinks of it in the rearview. Which suited him fine. Like most locals, he dug the closeness of it. People coexisted—mobile homes, beach shacks, stucco houses, redwood decks. Roses grew next to cacti, fuchsias next to Spanish bayonet. And up the street at the north end, bananas the fruit tree-ripening in bright blue bags.[1]

Long before I arrived in California, I knew something about La Conchita from the way it was described in a mystery novel written by Richard Barre. As seen through the eyes of Wil Hardesty (Barre's surf-riding detective, who made his home there), La Conchita was an unpretentious, slightly rough around the edges paradise that made me dream about someday living there too. As fate would have it, in 2002, while working at the College of William & Mary, I was offered a job at the University of California, Santa Barbara. The price tag for houses in Santa Barbara was astronomical, but I was not even looking there. I was excited to have found the perfect house for sale in La Conchita. My new colleagues and acquaintances were horrified by my choice of home sites, telling me that there had been a mudslide there in 1995. No one even mentioned that there had been major damage from mudslides in Malibu (home of the Hollywood rich and famous) in 1994, just about forty minutes south of La Conchita. As an outsider but obsessive researcher, I had become acquainted with this full range of natural disasters in the region covering a broad area, so it seemed rather strange to me that everyone was focusing all this negativity on tiny little La Conchita.

It became especially ironic when in an effort to thwart our La Conchita home-buying decision, we were shown a Santa Barbara home in a somewhat more affordable neighborhood where all the houses had burned down to the ground approximately two

Aerial view of La Conchita, November 1968. (*Rob Malone*)

years earlier. This option seemed a much more acceptable choice to my Santa Barbara colleagues. A community that had a mudslide seven years ago, which covered two blocks, was unacceptable, but a fire only two years earlier that burned down almost an entire neighborhood was acceptable. This made about as much sense as two plus two equaling five. I knew then there was a much more fascinating story behind the local perceptions of La Conchita and it had nothing to do with mudslides.

What is it about La Conchita that has continued to captivate me all these years? People talk about Serendipity and living here I have experienced much more than serendipity. This has been a place where coincidences collide. Sometimes, it is almost like I am living in the story I am writing. I know that I was destined to take on this research and write this book because too many things led me here. Even before I read the descriptions of La Conchita in Richard Barre's mystery *The Innocents*, living far away from California, I knew about this tiny little beach community that did not even rate a dot on most maps. It stuck in my mind because one of my favorite contemporary artists, Roger Brown, spent the last years of his life in La Conchita, creating a critically significant body of work. I greatly admired his work for most of my museum career. When I served as director of the Miami University Art Museum (Ohio), I would fly to Chicago to visit with the museum's major donors. When there was time, I would visit galleries and if I was lucky would see his work in exhibitions.

Even before my tenure at Miami University, I grew up in Lower Manhattan. When I walked into the Phyllis Kind Gallery in Soho, New York, in the early 1980s and saw Roger Brown's work for the first time, it knocked me out. I had never seen anything quite like it. To me, it seemed like the kind of the wild thinking I did but only gave related form to as a child. I never told anybody about those crazy little things I made in my pre-adolescent years, and you are not going to hear about them now.

When my La Conchita Exhibition was scheduled in California in 2010, the Roger Brown Study Collection simultaneously scheduled an exhibition of Roger Brown's La Conchita Paintings at the Hyde Park Art Center in Chicago and contacted me in La Conchita requesting a little assistance. If that is not enough of a coincidence, consider this. The first person to introduce herself to me as I moved into my La Conchita home was my next-door neighbor Phyllis Beck, who just happened to have been Roger Brown's hospice nurse. She was very fond of the artist. She told me that although she knew nothing about art and was nervous about being able to talk with a famous artist, right away, they found common ground in talking about gardening, and when he was conscious, he liked to hear Phyllis tell him about her collecting jaunts. Those were two of Phyllis's favorite pastimes, too. In fact, one might say most of this community has a serious addiction to these activities. Brown was very sick when Phyllis was called in, but when he was not sleeping, Brown enjoyed listening to Phyllis tell him about the out of the way places she found for unusual pottery for her plants. Phyllis and I were very close friends until her death in 2013.

Many people believe that there is no such thing as coincidences. There is always some concrete reason behind these related manifestations that seem to come from nowhere. As a research historian, I have tenaciously tried to find a concrete reason for all of the coincidences I have experienced since coming to La Conchita. I finally concluded that there is no concrete reason, *per se*; it is just that people with similar experiences are drawn to the unique fabric created by the extraordinary history of this community.

By virtue of what it is, La Conchita is a magnet for unconventional individuals and alternative lifestyles, and it provides fertile ground for creative innovation. There are other serendipitous stories in this book. You can choose to think that they are not coincidences. I will save the best for last. It may leave you shaking your heads or, if you are like me, just smile and be thankful that there is still a little magic like this in the world.

La Conchita had two mudslides in the history of the community's existence—one in 1995 and one in 2005, which was truly horrific. It was also a perfect storm. However, none of the reporting about either of the mudslides was accurate, especially the second one.

A treatise could be written on all of the errors in the major media articles and news segments on the mudslides. Terrible falsehoods about La Conchita gained a legitimate

Above left: Aftermath of the 2005 La Conchita Slide. (*Author's collection*)

Above right: Requiem for the Montecito debris slide, remnants of destroyed Montecito property on La Conchita Beach, 8 to 10 miles south of the disaster, 2018. (*Author's collection*)

focus, and the mudslides became the source of a constantly changing story of things that never happened, elaborated on, and passed on like the game of telephone by people who had never actually set foot in La Conchita. Sensational, grossly exaggerated journalism has taken place to discredit La Conchita ever since it began to thrive. Although there has not been any type of mud drop off or flooding here in fourteen years, many of the major newscasters never fail to mention their concern for our community every time it rains. I continue to wonder why they do not publicly worry about the far more horrific recent debris flow that shocked everyone last year in Montecito, the continual mudslides in Malibu, or the periodic giant rockslides around a number of the Ojai roads.

This deadly Montecito slide killed twenty-one people with two more missing and presumed dead. The force of this water-based torrent was so great that boulders and trees were propelled into the raging swell that totally destroyed more than 100 homes, sending the wreckage of homes, wildlife, and more down to the beach; the tides swept much of it out to sea, where it was deposited on other beaches some 8 miles south of the disaster. Yet, this disaster was quickly erased from the news and never reached many international outlets. In November and December 2018, massive mudslides near Las Flores Canyon closed down the Pacific Coast Highway for months, but news about these mudslides are not echoed in news stories whenever it rains.

Mudslides provided a convenient cover story. They just inspire sanctioned fear and skirt problematic issues like "prejudice," "discrimination," "the wrong class of people," or "This is not the type of community entitled to be on the Gold Coast of California." La Conchita is certainly not the only unstable place along coastal California, but it is the only community on the Gold Coast of California that is not affluent—still middle class and in part "blue collar" as it began even poorer almost 100 years ago. It remains integrated and has all kinds of mixed housing and people. La Conchita is an open community that accepts everyone. Money, social class, and entitlements are the credentials for acceptance in the rest of the Gold Coast, where extravagant beach houses and architect-designed compounds along the gated and famed beach communities are owned by Hollywood notables and corporate moguls. These are people who do not just influence the news, but they control it. As a research historian, I learned a long time ago that there is often a large gap between what we call "the truth," which tends to mean different things to different people, and what gets written up as the truth, which is often far from it. Fictionalized stories appear as truth in the mass media and then, especially in our electronic age, become history much sooner than in the past.

Looking back on 2018, from beginning to end, catastrophic events took place all around La Conchita. It may take our neighboring communities on the Gold Coast time to finally see, but the blinders will have to come off. Throughout 2018, Californians experienced some of the worst fires in the state's history. With massive destruction of magnificent national and state forest lands came the destruction of property and devastation. Following the Thomas Fire, with the loss of forestation and heavy rains, Montecito (the wealthiest community on the Gold Coast) suffered a massive and unexpected debris- and mudslide, with over 100 homes and buildings destroyed; over 300 more damaged; a tragic loss of twenty-one lives; two people still missing and presumed dead; Highway 101 (the main artery along the coast from LA to San Francisco) closed for 30 miles with more than 2 feet of mud and debris rushing from the mountains through Montecito and down to the ocean, with boulders tree trunks parts of housing; and even large dead wildlife landed on beaches, including our beach over 8 miles south of the catastrophe. The major news media has cited this catastrophe as the largest disaster in modern California history.

At the end of November 2018, in the aftermath of the tragic Woolsey Fire, Malibu once again experienced massive mudslides, further complicated by the fact that the city had not finished recovering from the destruction of the Woolsey Fire, and there were a number of people still missing and possibly buried in mud. In La Conchita, during all of these disasters, the streets were wet, but no mud came down from our mountainside. There was no flooding on any of the streets. La Conchita's name was not mentioned in conjunction with the word "mudslide" for the first time since we moved here in 2002. While we felt doubly blessed, since we were one of the few communities not touched by the fires either, we also deeply felt the tragedies around us. We had the memories of our own tragedy (even though it was fourteen years ago) as it is something you never forget. La Conchita residents with history here were really not surprised that we were okay, even with heavy rains and lack of constraining ground cover. Most of us knew it was the faulty irrigation from the ranch on top of our mountain that caused both of our mudslides. Once the ranch agreed to a settlement with the community, went bankrupt, and the former owner left, the problem ended because it was repaired by the new owner, who is well aware of his responsibility to this community.

For a while at least, those who believe La Conchitans are tarnishing the golden aura of the Coast have stopped casting stones. Whether it is because there is no mudslide potential here greater than anywhere else to use as a mask for the real motive or that they can finally see the truth is too soon to tell. We have all noticed that these major recent tragedies have already disappeared from the press, and our international friends who were barraged with sensationalist falsehoods about our own mudslide fourteen years ago never heard anything about the far larger disaster in Montecito at all. Perhaps in reading this book you will come to see that the negativity about La Conchita to a certain extent has come from media sources controlled by those with entitlement and influence. This is not conspiracy theory; it is fact. A significant mentor of mine, the late former senior scholar at the Smithsonian, Stephen E. Weil, kept reminding me that mass media and history today is only the "gossip of the winners."

This is a community totally unexpected among its neighbors on the Gold Coast of California. Most of the people who spread negative pronouncements about La Conchita have actually never set foot in this community. If they had, I do not believe they would be wasting energy on negative commentary. I thought a lot about that famous African proverb in writing this book: "Until the Lions have their historians, tales of the hunt will only glorify the hunters." This is why I have chosen to let our La Conchita "Lions" tell their own story about how they established an American Dream community almost 100 years ago and it has the right and is entitled to stay right where it is and be respected.

There is something about this place—a feeling people get—and it is why most people who live here feel so connected to it. This book could only tell the stories of a cross-section of the first generation to grow up in La Conchita and subsequent generations who lived here most or all their lives. In a way, they were self-selected by their longevity, willingness to participate, and most importantly by the documentation they saved over the years. What they contributed established the history and character of La Conchita beyond all of my hopes. That sense of community and the spirit it had when it began is still here. Several descendants of the first La Conchita Elders who settled this community without running water still live here.

La Conchita is a community where young people actually talk to old people. It is a place where your electrician lives two blocks over and your carpenter is down the street. It is a place where you can trade the Valencia oranges from your tree for avocados with your neighbor next door.

Your fisherman friend across the street will not only give you some of his catch, but he will fillet it and put it in plastic bags for you. People walking their dogs with coffee mugs in hand will meet in the middle of the street to talk face to face rather than on cell phones. Drivers and dogs will all be patient and do whatever is necessary until this vital human interaction is complete.

La Conchita is the home of surfers, master gardeners, retired teachers and engineers, writers, artists, musicians, horse whisperers, tango enthusiasts, and just about anyone else who loves the smell of the sea air and the mixture of botanical fragrances. Hopelessly eclectic at heart, it is a place where wild overflowing gardens encounter astonishingly large cacti. Housing ranges from creatively repurposed cottages to minimalist mansions. Any possibility can grow here; it is a different kind of paradise.

2

In the Beginning

What is now the community of La Conchita was originally part of the Rancho El Rincon. Early on, until 1923, this small beach settlement was named "Punta." Its larger coastal area was named "Punta Gorda," Spanish for "massive point," referring to the outstanding feature of this coastal area, a large rock promontory. A monk who stopped at the Mission Buenaventura in 1817 first mentioned the site. The history of the settlement of La Conchita is closely tied to developments in the Rincon Point area.

The name "The Rincon" was also routinely used to designate the area from Carpinteria's Rincon Point to Ventura's Sea Cliff. The "Rancho" was established through a historically significant land grant from Spain of 4,460 acres given to Teodoro Arrellanes in 1840. Arrellanes' daughter, Maria, married Dr. Matthew Biggs. The property was transferred to Dr. Biggs in 1855. From 1850 until 1873, when Ventura County was established, Punta Gorda was part of Santa Barbara County. During the 1860s, following a long period of draught, the record rainfall of 1868 produced major flooding throughout the county. It was during this time of climatic calamity that major portions of the great old ranchos were subdivided and sold off by heirs to an increasing number of arriving Anglos. The Homesteading Act of 1862 had brought many adventurous newcomers to settle in California.

Levi Gould Stanchfield (born in Leeds, Maine, in 1858) established a ranch at Punta Gorda in 1875, where he raised sheep, grew lima beans, and built a ranch house at Mussel Rock. Stanchfield sold the property to Charles. E. Ablett in 1879. Born in England, Ablett was well-known as a druggist in Santa Barbara and a key figure in the homesteading activity of the Punta Gorda area from the 1880s onward. At this time, the La Conchita section of the Southern Pacific railroad was almost completed, and the village of Punta was established. Among the founding families of Punta were the Callis from Kentucky; the Mullins from Charlotte, Prince Edward Island, Canada; and the Gaynors from Ireland. Various members of these families made lasting contributions to the region for over sixty years. The dominant occupation began to shift from farming to oil drilling in the 1880s, which was firmly established by the Punta Gorda Oil Company in 1890.

Greetings from CALIFORNIA

808:-OIL WELLS ALONG COAST HIGHWAY BETWEEN
VENTURA AND SANTA BARBARA, CALIFORNIA

Greetings from California (with oil wells), historic postcard. (*Jeff Ross*)

Punta Annual Hill Climb, 1912–20. (*Jeff Ross*)

In the early 1900s, Punta's long natural slope down to the highway became the perfect site for what was billed as the Punta Annual Hill Climb. There were heats for both motorcycles and cars in this annual event. Prior to the establishment of the village of Punta, the coastal area was named "Punta Gorda." Punta was the name given to La Conchita from its earliest days, when it was a stop for the pony express, then a stagecoach stop and a post office. It only became known as La Conchita after the failure of the beachfront development in 1923. Strangely enough, although it has been called La Conchita ever since, Ventura County only made that official in 1996.

From 1880 to 1916, a U.S. post office was sited in Punta, and Punta Gorda served as a stop for both the stagecoach and the railroad. Charles E. Ablett served as the first postmaster. In 1883, the Rincon school district was established and classes were first held in the home of Robert Callis with nine pupils in attendance. The 1883 census listed seventeen children living in Punta. In 1890, the name was changed to the Punta Gorda school district, and the first school structure was built in the village—Punta Gorda School, whose foundation can still be seen in the orchard across from Carpinteria Street in La Conchita.

The Ventura County register of 1890, as well as the Rincon district electoral records from 1900 to 1916, reflects a rich cultural mix of Anglo and Hispanic residents in Punta and the Rincon area. The school was replaced by a more substantial building in 1935. Robert Bates became involved with the school and sought the resources of a most creative teacher, Miss Bessie Davison; for seventeen years together, they developed an

The first Punta Gorda School House built in 1912. (*Ventura County Archives*)

innovative and progressive program well beyond its time. The Punta Gorda School had a major impact on the development of La Conchita.

Robert Bates and Andrew Bailard purchased land in La Conchita in hopes of finding oil in the area. Andrew Bailard had purchased 500 acres of land in Carpinteria in 1898. This enterprise was to fail financially. As noted in the memoirs of Edward Bates, from 1910 until the late 1920s, the beach area of the Rincon was looked on as more of a liability than an asset. Unsuccessful drilling for water also began in earnest at this time. Edward C. Ramelli bought land that had a resort hotel called the Mussel Rock Inn and property in La Conchita at the water's edge in 1923.

His brother, Milton, was a civil engineer and surveyor. He laid out the first nineteen homes and called it "La Conchita del Mar." The following May, Milton Ramelli laid out 327 more lots on a dozen 40-foot streets on the uphill side of the railroad tracks. La Conchita del Mar was promoted as an affordable seaside paradise with lots available starting at $200, which included oil rights. It was called a "beach with a future." Milton Ramelli also subdivided the sixty-six-lot community of Mussel Shoals in 1924 on land owned by the Hickey Brothers. He also developed Solimar Beach on leased land ten years later.

Successful oil drilling off of Mussel Rock began in 1927. Oil workers leased rental property in La Conchita. A mild interest in beach property began to grow in the early 1930s. However, despite oil fields producing in Sea Cliff and elsewhere on the Rincon, no oil was discovered in La Conchita. The fresh water promised to all lots never materialized either.

It is most important to understand that "La Conchita" is Spanish for little shell, which was first used as the name for a spur on the Southern Pacific railroad line in the 1880s, and it was a name generally used to describe a broader area then the present-day village. During this time until 1923, the small beach settlement was named "Punta" and the street names still carried today (San Fernando, Ojai, Bakersfield, Carpinteria, etc.) commemorated the hometown areas of the railroad workers who settled in the town while building the Southern Pacific line. The name change and designated area then known as La Conchita are crucially important to any understanding of the region today and its geological history. Up through the 1930s as historically documented, the area from Bates Road down to Mussel Shoals (then known as Mussel Rock) was referred to as La Conchita. This fact has led to much misrepresentation of the landslide history of the village now known as La Conchita. In fact, prior to the 1995 landslide, there have been no documented landslides in the present-day La Conchita community. All of the prior landslide activity, including the infamous 1909 and 1911 railroad landslides with loss of lives, took place north of the present-day village. A careful study of the photographs of these historic landslides provides proof of this beyond any doubt. All of the La Conchita Elders have testified that during all the years they lived in La Conchita, there have never been any mud- or landslides in the community.

In 1923, due to unverified research, millionaire investors lost their bankrolls trying to create a seaside paradise called "La Conchita del Mar." Unfortunately, they could not find water or oil as promised for each lot. The plan turned out to be a disaster, with the land considered worthless, and the project was abandoned. It was just that simple twist of fate that allowed a group of Filipino farmers, Mexican railroad workers, and poor white oil workers to be able to cheaply buy up this property and build a

La Conchita del Mar Ads, *Ventura Star*, 1923.

La Conchita del Mar Ads, *Ventura Star*, 1924.

community where the rich investors failed. This new group of integrated landowners, a number of whom started studying for their American citizenship, bonded together across ethnic boundaries and built a little utopian community where everyone was equal and prejudice simply did not exist. They took their model from this country's founding documents and the American Dream of freedom and equality for all. Some of the original investors in La Conchita del Mar had actually encouraged members of this group to purchase the cheap land. They did not quite believe it would develop into the thriving community it did. How could these people with no resources build a community with no water when people with wealth and resources could not make it work? It was all about orientation—these were poor people who learned how to do practically anything with nothing. Owning land in America was the impossible dream they thought was beyond their reach and would never give it up.

The photos of the two "founding matriarchs" of La Conchita (on the opposite page) are rare. Jesse Gallardo was the wife of Joseph, who build the first house in La Conchita in 1927 that still stands. The couple and their relatives came directly from Mexico and found work with the railroad. Jesse had eleven children. Like most of the Filipino immigrants of this period, Pelagia Dacayana came to this country by way of Hawaii. She outlived three husbands and, sadly, one daughter.

Without water, this enterprising community of people built cisterns and had water delivered from Lake Casitas to supply what rain failed to provide. They grew drought-tolerant food sources like lima beans and cactus fruits, and they fished in a bay teeming with all kinds of nourishment. My La Conchita Elders all told of wading into the water and putting their hands in the sand, grabbing hold of lobsters, crabs, and clams. It was also discovered that La Conchita's land was far from worthless; in fact, it was unique. Everything and anything could grow in its unique microclimate, from banana trees to rare orchids. This hard-working racial mix of people who now had a small piece of the American Dream were never forgiven by those who had everything and saw a threat to their exclusive life style and reputation on the Gold Coast of CA.

Against all odds, this group with little more than belief, hope, and strong will achieved their impossible dream of having land of their own. La Conchita became a unique, multicultural, working-class coastal neighborhood. A rich mix of ethnic and cultural elements shaped the character of this community. For 100 years, La Conchita has ignored the slights from its affluent neighbors and continues to have a distinct sense of place, one that welcomes cultural difference, appreciates individuality, and embraces creative possibilities.

Above left: Jesse Gallardo and her sisters in Mexico, 1918. (*Eleanor Gallardo*)

Above right: Pelagia Dacayana and her godparents in Hawaii, 1920. (*Chet Dacayana*)

3

Dreams of Paradise

The Punta Gorda Land and Oil Company was established in 1900. By 1930, there were a dozen or so families living in small cottages at the foot of the hill. Lima beans grew on either side of the community and the land gently sloped down to the shore broken only by the railroad tracks and the two-lane old Rincon Highway. Catering to the oil workers as well as the weekenders and summer vacation people, beachfront properties included a restaurant, tavern, and a short fishing wharf. Rudy Scheidman commissioned *La Conchita*, a 1930s oil painting by artist Victor Nikol. It gives one of the best overall views of cottages and beachfront amenities in La Conchita, a thriving seaside community prior to World War II.

Pete Richardson came to La Conchita in 1928 when he was two years old. He was suffering from terminal cancer when I interviewed him, but he would take his walker out on the streets of La Conchita as much as he could for as long as he could. He allowed me to walk with him on occasion. He took pride in the fact that the names of the streets in La Conchia were named for the home towns of the oil men who first came to drill oil here. His father, Harry Richardson, was an oil worker who dug the first oil well in Mussel Shoals (then known as Mussel Rock). At that time, Richardson remembered (he has since passed away) his family as having the only "real house in La Conchita," an adobe whose foundation can still be found just south of town. His father put up two water tanks for water to be delivered by truck.

It made Mr. Richardson furious when people claimed the two mudslides of recent years (and the only mudslides in La Conchita as long as he had been living there) were caused by underground spring water in the mountains. He stated:

> Hell, there never was any water or oil, for that matter! I'm 80, and I've been here for 78 years, there never was any water. Everybody was looking for water—the oil companies, with all their money—the developers, who invested so much here—if there was any

Above: La Conchita by Victor Nikol (1930), oil painting. (*Jack and Karen Oren*)

Right: Pete Richardson, *c.* 1930. (*Yan Richardson*)

Above: Gallardo House, 2018—for sale. (*Author's collection*)

Below: Oil wells in the Pacific looking south from the Old Paved Highway. (*Jeff Ross*) (*Eleanor Gallardo Ramey*)

> water anywhere, don't you think they would have found it? It was just irresponsible irrigation that caused our slides![1]

The Gallardo Clan

Author's Notes from Interviews with Eleanor Gallardo Ramey

Joseph and Jesse Gallardo emigrated from Mexico in 1919. Eleanor stated:

> My father came to California with the equivalent of 25 cents in his pocket and no prospects at all. He went to work for the railroad watching and clearing the lonely stretch of track between the Santa Barbara County line and Mussel Rock (shoals) and built one of the first permanent houses in La Conchita in 1927 (the oldest house still in existence).[2]

Above left: Nash, Abel, and Louie Galladro: the oldest three boys of the Gallardo's eleven children, *c*. 1928.

Above right: Joseph and Jesse Gallardo, *c*. 1927. (*Eleanor Gallardo Ramey*)

Gallardo House front view, 1927.

Gallardo House side view, 1927.

Abel, Rosie, and Louie Gallardo. (*Eleanor Gallardo Ramey*)

Above left: Eleanor Gallardo in the 1950s. (*Eleanor Gallardo Ramey*)

Above right: April 29, 1945: Gallardo Family Armed Services Homecoming. *Top row from left*: Ted and Joseph; *middle row from left*: Abel (Army), Jesse, and Louie (Navy); *bottom row from left*: Marilyn and Rosie. (*Eleanor Gallardo Ramey*)

An intercultural gathering, La Conchita style, *c.* 1939. *From the left*: no. 1: Frank Hughes, (below) Rudy Scheidman, no. 2 Pauline Talaugon, no. 3 Shirley Dacayana, no. 4 Pelagia Dacayana. (*Ben Dacayana*)

Rudy Scheidman was a well-known figure in La Conchita, where he co-owned the Mussel Rock Inn with Frank Ragamey on the beach at Mussel Rock (today known as Mussel Shoals) from 1931 to 1935. When the highway was widened to three lanes in 1935, the restaurant had to be moved to the beach at La Conchita and was renamed as Frank and Rudy's. World War II put the restaurant out of business as travel through La Conchita all but stopped. It closed in 1942. Scheidman loved Filipino food and generally managed to get himself invited to various family banquets and events. He also was recognized for teaching many of the young boys in the community how to surf.

One of the things my number one informant, Eleanor Gallardo Ramey, said that I would hear over and over again in all of my interviews with people who grew up in La Conchita was that she never knew that there were "people who did not like Mexicans until she left La Conchita," and she was right. Punta Gorda School was always a thoroughly integrated school, and La Conchita was always a thoroughly integrated community through the 1930s to the 1950s and beyond, at a time when this was certainly not the case in the surrounding areas of California (or the rest of the country for that matter. Each one of my informants would tell me that they never knew anything about prejudice until they left La Conchita!

People would say to me when I was outside of La Conchita "How can you live there with no running water? I would think to myself, I'd rather live without running water than live with all of their prejudice and hatred," Eleanor Gallardo Ramey stated.

4

The Filipino Community in La Conchita

From the 1930s onward, La Conchita became a center of the thriving Filipino community on the Central Coast. The Filipino Cultural Center on lower State Street in Santa Barbara was established and initially run by families living in La Conchita. Many of the most prominent Filipino families in the area today began their lives as Americans in La Conchita and have enriched the cultural fabric of the Central California region. The Talaugons and Gallardos have maintained a presence in La Conchita since its founding. The Dacayanas have only left in the past twenty years or so. Filipino and Mexican people have been consistently enriching the La Conchita community since its founding.

The Filipino Community of La Conchita

Talaugon/Razo Families of La Conchita (Submitted by B. Talaugon-Dunn)

Magdalena Razo was a survivor of the Mexican Revolution. Her brother rode with Pancho Villa. She emigrated to California with her mother and married Francisco Razo in Los Angeles, California. They moved to La Conchita in 1939 with their children: Catalina, Mariano, and Consuelo. Southern Pacific Railroad transferred Francisco to night watchman at Rincon Point. Children born in La Conchita include Efren, Sara, and Amalia Razo. Their young son, Efren, was killed by a train in La Conchita. Their daughter, Catalina, married Federico Talaugon. Two granddaughters, Flora F. Razo and B. Talaugon-Dunn, still live in La Conchita.

Federico Arnado Talaugon (Peding), his wife Asuncion, and their family leased a large house and land from the Gaynor family ranch between La Conchita and the Rincon. They moved there in 1932 and were part of the growing Filipano community that seemed to gravitate to La Conchita as an opportune area for their first American home. Many leased land to farm from the large ranches of the region. Federico Talaugon and his three brothers—Andres, Severo, and Paulino—worked on the Gaynor property until around 1950

Federico A. Talaugon, Sr., at Gaynor Ranch, *c.* 1930s. (*B. Talaugon-Dunn*)

Magdalena and Francisco Razo on La Conchita Beach in 1924. (*B. Talaugon-Dunn*)

when most of the family either moved to neighboring La Conchita or Carpinteria. Federico Talaugon would later marry Catalina Herrera Razo, who he met in La Conchita.

"I have only the fondest of memories of my years in La Conchita. There was no prejudice; there were no race issues. People all helped and learned from each other. It was a beautiful place & time."[3]

Federico Arnado Talaugon (nicknamed "Peding Talaugon") was born in Putat, Tuburan, Cebu Island, Philippines, in 1902. In 1917, he stowed away on a ship to Hawaii with a cousin. While in Hawaii, he worked on a sugar cane plantation on Oahu. He located his older brother, Paulino Talaugon (nicknamed "Ninong") while attending a Saturday night boxing match at a nearby plantation; Ninong was in the ring. Peding and Ninong left Hawaii for California.

Later, their younger brothers, Andres and Severo (nicknamed "Lolong"), joined them. Andres died of tuberculosis and is buried in the Chinese section of the Ivy Lawn Cemetery in Ventura, California. The brothers spent time in the Stockton and Guadalupe area and eventually settled and farmed (Talaugon Brothers' Produce) in La Conchita in 1932. His cousin, Loy Alpiña, also resided in La Conchita with his wife, Paulina.

Peding married Asuncion Villiano in 1932. Asuncion had a daughter, Gloria, who was later adopted by Peding. From 1932 to 1952, Peding was employed by the Gaynor family. In 1932, Asuncion and Peding had a son, Federico A. Talaugon, Jr. In 1937, Peding

Above left: Asuncion Villiano Talaugon Wisco, *c.* 1931. (*Federico Talaugon, Jr.*)

Above right: On board the *President Hoover* steamship to the Philippines: Federico Talaugon, Jr., and Federico Talaugon, Sr., 1937. (*B. Talaugon-Dunn*)

and Asuncion divorced. Stanley Shepard of the Carpinteria Shepard Family became a patron of Peding and sent him to agriculture school, where he honed in on the skill of grafting avocado trees. After World War II, Peding developed the McArthur avocado. To his disappointment, the avocado was the size of a grapefruit and the seed two-third the size of the fruit. In 1952, Peding married Catalina Herrera Razo (twenty-five years his junior), the eldest daughter of La Conchita residents Francisco and Magdalena Razo. They have two surviving daughters, Rebecca M. Venuti and B. Talaugon-Dunn.

B. Talaugon-Dunn

Federico Arnado Talaugon, Jr. (a.k.a. Dick Talaugon), was born in Ventura, California, in 1932 to Asuncion and Federico Talaugon. He graduated from Long Beach State with an engineering degree. In 1958, he married Nora Ventura, the only daughter of Felipe Ventura, who was known as the "Green Onion King." They had five children. He was employed by Lockheed's Propulsion Center in Redlands, California, while residing in Riverside. In 1961, he moved to San Jose after being transferred by Lockheed. In 1998, he retired from Lockheed in management as senior staff engineer and purchased a home in Santa Paula, where he currently resides with his wife, Nora.

Beatrice V. Talaugon-Dunn (a.k.a. Bea Dunn) was the youngest daughter of Catalina and Federico Talaugon, half-sister to Federico Talaugon, Jr., and was born in Ventura, California, in 1955. She attended school in Santa Barbara and Ventura and was a member of the volleyball team for Santa Barbara High School. An avid local La Conchita surfer, she was a member of the original "La Conchita Surfergirls." She was raised

Left: Federico A. Talaugon, Sr., and Catalina Herrera Razo-Talaugon. (*B. Talaugon-Dunn*)

Opposite above: The Ventura Associated Farmers softball team, first organized by the Talaugon brothers, *c.* 1939. Those identified are second and third from the top left are Paulino (Ninong) Talaugon and Severo (Lulong) Talaugon. Second from the top right is Lauriano (Aloui) Alpiña and fourth from the right is Venancio Dacayana. In the bottom row, third and fourth from the left are Federico (Peding) Talaugon, Sr., and Bundy. (*B. Talaugon-Dunn*)

Opposite below: Federico Arnado Talaugon, Sr., Federico Adnado Talaugon, Jr., and Beatrice Talaugon-Dunn. (*B. Talaugon-Dunn*)

ASSOCIATED
FARMERS
VENTURA

primarily in La Conchita as well as in the Carpinteria, Santa Barbara, and Montecito. Ms. Talaugon-Dunn received her AA degree from Ventura College, Paralegal Certificate from UCSB's Paralegal Program, and eventually graduated from the University of California at Santa Barbara with a degree in law and society. She currently resides in La Conchita with her husband, Jerry Dunn.

THE DACAYANA FAMILY OF LA CONCHITA

Born in the Philippines, Venancio Dacayana and Pelagia Putane met and married in Pahoa, Hawaii, in the 1920s as contract farm workers on a sugar plantation. She had emigrated from Antiquera, Bohol; he was from Cebu. They came to California and eventually settled in La Conchita where they farmed their land and cared for their young family. Tragically, their oldest daughter, Shirley, died in 1941 from a pulmonary illness; in 1948, Venancio also died, leaving Pelagia to raise the four surviving children. She later married longtime family friend Bartolome Rabino. After Bartolome's death in the 1980s, she married Claudio Recurba. Pelagia died in 1996 at the age of eighty-nine.

Venancio and Pelagia's four remaining children grew to adulthood in La Conchita and followed diverse and successful career paths.

Pelagia Dacayana (center) holds the first-place softball trophy won by Venancio Dacayana's team, 1930s. The team was composed mostly of truck farmers from La Conchita, Carpinteria, and Santa Barbara. To the right of Pelagia Putane Dacayana is Pauline Alpenia, Shirley Dacayana and (directly behind them) Venancio Dacayana and Nenong Alpenia. The children seated in front from left to right are (second from left): Jackie Alpenia, Josie Dacayana, Chester Dacayana, Bobby Dacayana, with two unidentified childern at each end. (*Chet Dacayana*)

Above left: Bobby, Josie, and Chester Dacayana, *c.* late 1930s. (*Chet Dacayana*)

Above right: Pelagia Putane and Bartulome Rabino. (*Chet Dacayana*)

Below: Shirley Dacayana on horseback. (*Ben Dacayana*)

Chester (Chet) Dacayana was a 1952 Cal Poly graduate. He retired in 1992 as the district operations manager for the Ventura Unified School District, where he served for thirty-five years. Chet Dacayana was also a highly respected sports official for many years and the first inductee to the Ventura County Sports Hall of Fame. Chester and his late wife, Jan, had five children—Jana, Lalani, Tony, Sara, and Cara. They were also involved in the Ventura County foster parent program for thirty years. He was also a longtime volunteer for the Ventura County Fair, where he was active in the 4H, FFA, and home arts programs. Chester remained active in community life after retiring to Port Oreford Oregon, where he died in 2009 at age eighty.

Josephine (Dacayana) Cabugos attended Immaculate Heart College and Queen of Angels Nursing School in Hollywood. She served thirty-three years as a registered nurse at St. Francis Hospital in Santa Barbara, volunteered for medical humanitarian missions, and participated in numerous non-profit fundraising efforts. A prominent leader in the Filipino community, upon her death in 1999, she was lauded by the *Santa Barbara News-Press* for her many accomplishments. She and her late husband, Teofilo ("Ted") Cabugos, had four children; their oldest son, Theodore, was lost at sea in 2000 while kayaking off the Santa Barbara coast. Their daughter, Mujiba, and sons, Perry and Nicholas, live in Santa Barbara.

Robert Dacayana attended Ventura College and became a highly regarded professional in the Santa Barbara hospitality industry, where he managed the famed Plow and Angel at San Ysidro Ranch for many years. He retired from the Olive Mill Bistro, a noted Montecito restaurant. His fine tenor voice was popular with patrons of both establishments, where he received numerous requests to sing. Today, Robert and his wife, Sonja, live in Carpinteria. He took up woodworking in retirement, and his fine handmade furniture and other objects are much sought after by friends and family. Bobby died in 2012.

Benjamin Dacayana, the youngest of Pelagia and Venancio's children, became an engineer for Hughes and Honeywell. He was one of the developers of a Hughes satellite that was exhibited for many years at the Smithsonian Air and Space Museum. Benjamin and his wife, Yvon, retired in San Diego County, where he is a volunteer pilot with the Civil Air Patrol flying search and rescue missions. He also pursues other community activities and is still playing his guitar at age sixty-seven. As a college student, he performed in a Carpinteria surf band, which was offered a contract by a major record label; his love of music rubbed off on his daughter, Melora Dacayana Hutton, who performs in musical theater in Southern California and Las Vegas. Melora's maternal grandfather was Charles H. Munro, the Southern Pacific's last agent at the Carpinteria railroad station.

The Dacayanas were one of the founding families of the Filipino Community Association of Santa Barbara, which has owned and operated its building on State Street in downtown Santa Barbara since the 1950s. Pelagia Dacayana was involved at the inception and in the acquisition of the property. Daughter Josephine and her husband served on the board of directors; their sons, Perry and Nicholas (grandchildren of Venancio and Pelagia Dacayana), are among today's leaders of the organization.

Above left: Chet Dacayana. (*Ben Dacayana*)

Above right: Pelagia Dacayana (left) and Josephine Dacayana (second from right) with friends in La Conchita, *c.* early 1940s. (*Ben Dacayana*)

5

THE PUNTA GORDA SCHOOL AND ROBERT BATES:
PROGRESSIVE AND INNOVATIVE EDUCATION

This chapter documents the history of the Punta Gorda School District prior to its golden years with Robert Bates, Bessie Davison, and Margaret Hughes.

Punta Gorda School class of 1930 is among the earliest surviving class pictures after the establishment of the community of La Conchita. The children of families working for the ranches on the Rincon, as well as those living in La Conchita, all attended the Punta Gorda School. In the background is teacher Miss Bessie Davison. On the far left, second row, is Ignacio "Nash" Gallardo, the oldest son of Joseph and Jesse Gallardo. Second from the right in the first row is the Gallardo's second son, Abel. In the first row, first on the left and second on the right are the Ota girls, Hanei and Masai, whose father (Tom Ota) worked as a foreman and leased land to farm from the Bates family's Rincon del Mar Ranch. On the far right in the second row is Teresa Ramirez, whose father worked for the Southern Pacific Railroad as a trackwalker.

The history of the Punta Gorda School goes back to the very beginnings of the community. By the early 1880s, there were at least three families ranching in Punta, as La Conchita was known back then. Along with the ranchers and their wives and children, there was the usual assortment of farmhands, laborers, and the like. Many of these also had families. In 1883, seventeen children were living here, eight or nine of school age. Due to Punta's remoteness from Ventura and Carpenteria, someone figured it was a good idea to start a school. The August 11, 1883, edition of the *Ventura Free Press* notes the establishment of the Rincon school district (later changed to Punta Gorda school district) on August 1. The first classes were held in November at the homestead of Robert A. Callis (1843–1905), a noted Ventura County pioneer. This was located south of Punta, near Las Sauces Creek. The first teacher was C. M. Drake.

Ventura County, although considering it to be a small district, granted funding to build a schoolhouse. The whole site chosen was 1 mile north in the northwest corner of the avocado orchard across from present day Carpenteria Ave. Early photographs show a well-built wood frame structure of about 20 feet by 30 feet with tongue-in-groove siding

Punta Gorda School Class of 1930 is among the earliest surviving class pictures after the establishment of the community of La Conchita. (*Eleanor Gallardo Ramey*)

and a shingle roof. It served the community for around fifty years until replaced in 1935 by a new building. The old schoolhouse was moved around to different locations over the years, and it used to house both people and livestock at various times. It wound up sitting in a corner of the oilfields at Seacliff, after it had been donated to the county as a historic building. Unfortunately, by then, it was riddled with termites and in quite bad shape. It was demolished in the late 1990s.

The new building was somewhat larger, with stucco walls and a tile roof typical of the mission-style architecture that was popular in California at the time. It sat on a substantial concrete foundation and had its own cistern as a water supply. Inside was an office, restrooms, a large single classroom, and a smaller room in the back. The floor was covered with linoleum. There was a small asphalt playground with a swing set, and the whole lot was surrounded by a post and rail fence. Completing the picture was a flagpole and a large eucalyptus tree that served as a landmark for many years. It was quite a modern building for the time, although not lavish. Its career as a schoolhouse would be far shorter than its predecessor.

Home movies taken in the mid-thirties show a largely happy, culturally mixed group of children playing in front of a well-kept schoolhouse. Many of the kids that attended during that period were still in the community in the 1990s. Classes continued until the early 1940s, when America entered the war. After the war, Ventura County's school district had taken over and decided to bus the children of La Conchita down to Ventura for classes. Throughout the history of the Punta Gorda School, attendance was seldom more than twelve kids, and it made sense to send them to schools in Ventura rather than operate one in such a remote location; so ended a sixty-year tradition. Nothing official was ever written about the mother and three girls who lived in the school for more than a year (1848–9) until the following chapter. Contrary to Ventura County accounts, the building did not stand empty. Numerous groups in the area used it for meetings and organizational events; church groups used it for choir practice. The county was in a hurry to claim it for its own purposes. Residents would have liked it to stay. In the early 1950s, the schoolhouse was moved to an elementary school campus on Santa Clara Street in Ventura. It has since disappeared. This material was found in numerous sources (including Bates Family Archives and interviews) but is also publicly accessible through the Ventura County Historical Society Archives.

On September 2, 2006, Eleanor Gallardo Ramey came over with a big box of photos—forty-eight of them to be exact, and what was most amazing about looking at Eleanor's photos was the La Conchita history lesson she gave me. My house was across the street and three doors up from the house her father built in 1927, the oldest existing house in La Conchita. Most vivid in her memories were her years at the Punta Gorda School. As we looked at each picture, without hesitation, she could name every single student in these school pictures from the 1930s and tell me great stories about all the school's creative activities and their amazing teacher, Miss Davison, who managed to teach all six grades. She also talked at length about Mrs. Hughes and Mr. Robert Bates, and how both of these people made all sorts of things possible for children from relatively poor families.

Punta Gorda School and its students, *c.* 1933–4. This building replaced a significantly smaller wooden structure built around 1912. (*Eleanor Gallardo Ramey*)

ROBERT W. BATES

La Conchita and the Rincon were originally part of the Rancho El Rincon, a historically significant land grant from Spain of 4,460 acres given to Teodoro Arrellanes in 1840. Dr. Matthew Biggs received the property through marriage in 1855. Dr. C. E. Bates and Dr. Benigno Guiterrez bought out Dr. Biggs and jointly owned the ranch until 1903–4. In 1889, Mary Carmen (Chatta) and her husband, Dr. Ruben Hill, inherited about 50 acres at Rincon Point. The Hills made their homestead on the west side of the creek. The Bates-Guiterrez partnership dissolved. After the death of Dr. Rubin Hill, the Rincon Point land east of the creek was transferred to the Bates family. Dr. C. E. Bates was an English doctor drawn to the California gold rush. He later practiced medicine in Santa Barbara. Robert W. Bates, returned home from military service in Europe during World War I and joined his father Edward Bates in running the Rincon del Mar Ranch along with his brothers, Edward and Stacy.

Robert Bates and his French wife Juliette Bates loved the coastal area of the Rincon and all the children of the area. It was not surprising that he became invested in the Punta Gorda School or that he helped a number of the families he got to know personally by paying their medical bills and seeing to other crucial needs. He really did make the difference in many lives and some seventy-five years later there were quite a few former students or members of their families that made it to the opening of the La Conchita: Reclaiming its Past exhibition to pay their respects.

The one-room, one-teacher Punta Gorda School had been around since 1892, and while there is no way to definitively prove it since record-keeping was spotty at best, it was possibly the first integrated public school in California. Robert Bates was a local landowner and philanthropist who had been an investor in the ill-fated La Conchita del Mar project. He also was a Utopian, interested in La Conchita, democratic ideals, and education as a key to success. He joined the school board in the early 1930s and became convinced that the way out of poverty was education. He invested his own funds into educational programs and equipment at the Punta Gorda School. Working closely with the vice president of the board, Mrs. Margaret Hughes, and the amazing Mis Bessie Davison, they developed an advanced curriculum that was miles ahead of the other public schools of the time. Although the 1937 and '38 copies of *Whisperings* are now too deteriorated to reproduce writing sample details, enough can be seen with magnification to show that second and third graders were writing in script and their compositions were at around a 6th Grade level, according to several educators who have examined them. In addition to that, students at the Punta Gorda School during the "Bates years" also had an international or multicultural education, unheard of at this time. The children would have international pageants where they would learn about and celebrate the cultures of other countries. Their curriculum also included music and art. They even had health classes.

The school was so important to the children of La Conchita, many of whom came to school barefoot; it changed their lives. A number of people who came to the opening of the La Conchita exhibition in 2010 attended the Punta Gorda school some seventy-five years earlier. Those I spoke with told me the school changed their lives and that they never would have the profession they have now if it had not been for the Punta Gorda School.

The guardian angels of Punta Gorda School were the school's generous benefactor and president of the school board, Mr. Robert W. Bates; the dedicated Mrs. Margaret Hughes, a member of the school board who lived in La Conchita and subsequently became president of the board when Bates' term ended; and the inspiring teacher Miss Bessie Davison. However, for all of the many children who attended the Punta Gorda schoolhouse, it is Miss Bessie Davison and her outstanding creativity and abilities as a teacher that remain most vivid in the memories of those who passed through the school doors over seventy years ago.

The musical notes image is just one example of the creative and enjoyable forms of education taught by Bessie Davison at the Punta Gorda School. The school had classes in music and art as well as a quality liberal arts core. Children learned how to read music and how to play a musical instrument. The school had a band that was quite well-known throughout the school district and would travel to play at other schools. Robert Bates supplied funds for band uniforms.

The graduating class of 1938 is a great picture of four close friends from very different ethnic and cultural backgrounds who have known each other all their lives and see no differences between them. Each of them would experience a rude awakening when the left La Conchita to live in the outside world.

The "Guardian Angels" of Punta Gorda School, Margaret Hughes & Bessie Davison were the School's generous benefactor and President of the School Board, Mr. Robert W. Bates & the dedicated Mrs. Margaret Hughes, a member of the school board who lived in La Conchita and subsequently became President of the Board when R. W. Bates term ended. (*Eleanor Gallardo Ramey*)

Right: Robert W. Bates. (*Carpinteria Valley Museum of History*)

Below: Punta Gorda School students dressed as musical notes, *c.* 1938. *From the left*: Dorothy Musick, Chester Dacayana, Ted Gallardo, Jesse Wilson, Jack Alpiña, Ed Musick, Dan Ruano, Charlie Gallardo, and Charlotte Gallardo. (*Eleanor Gallardo Ramey*)

Above left: Punta Gorda School graduation class of 1938. *From the left*: Shirley Dacayana, Ellen Valhbruch, Eleanor Gallardo, and Edward Musick. (*Eleanor Gallardo Ramey*)

Above right: *Whisperings* 1937 cover. (*Chet Dacayana*)

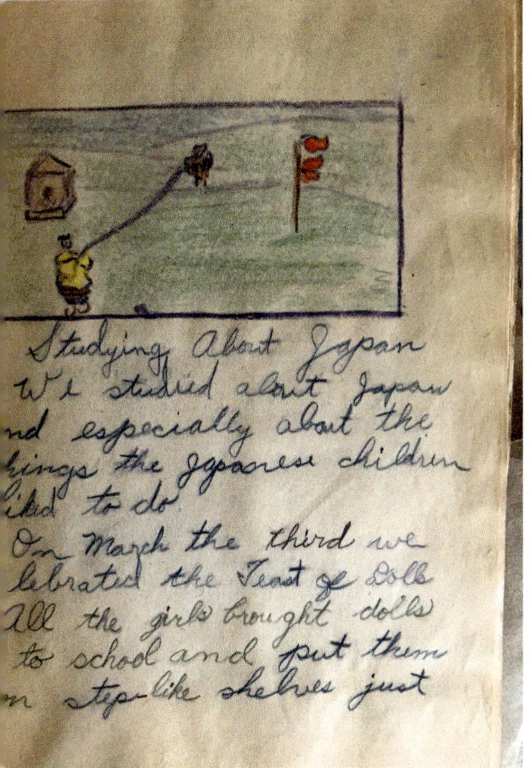

Studying About Japan
We studied about Japan
nd especially about the
hings the Japanese children
iked to do
On March the third we
lebrated the Feast of Dolls
All the girls brought dolls
to school and put them
n step-like shelves just

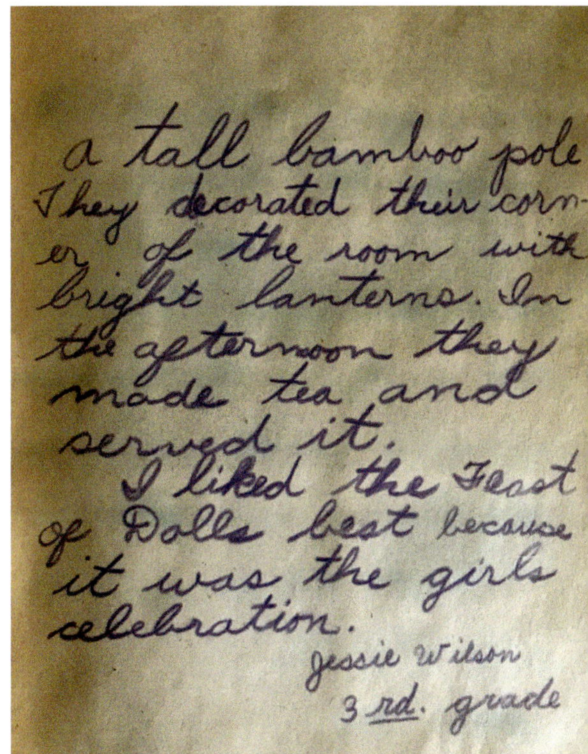

a tall bamboo pole
They decorated their corner of the room with
bright lanterns. In
the afternoon they
made tea and
served it.
I liked the Feast
of Dolls best because
it was the girls
celebration.
Jessie Wilson
3 rd. grade

Above left and right: Whispering 1938 issue: a sample from Jesse Wilson's report on the Japanese Doll Festival.

Right: Whisperings 1938 theme: "Pacific Playmates." In 1938, the pageant was titled "Our Pacific Playmates" and is detailed in one of the handwritten reports included within. (*Chet Dacayana*)

Above: The Punta Gorda School international costume pageants every year as part of the curriculum study in world history and cultures. (*Eleanor Gallardo Ramey*)

Below left: Mary Ruano and Dorothy Musick posed as Japanese ladies. (*Eleanor Gallardo Ramey*)

Below right: Jesse Wilson performing as a Hawaiian dancer. (*Eleanor Gallardo Ramey*)

In 1938, the pageant was titled "Our Pacific Playmates" and is detailed in one of the handwritten reports included in *Whisperings*, a student-created yearbook. The 1937 and 1938 editions of *Whisperings* are surviving examples of Punta Gorda School's annual student reviews, which consisted of student reports on various school activities throughout the year and were illustrated with student drawings.

During our many conversations, both by phone and e-mail, Chet Dacayana served as the author's assistant, making contacts and looking up old friends to provide answers to my many questions, up until two weeks prior to his death October 2010. He was a special person and is dearly missed.

Chet told me many things about his family's gratitude to Robert W. Bates. His father, Venancio Dacayana, told him how "R. W. Bates took him under his wing and took him to a few land auctions. He told my Dad if he ever wanted to succeed in life, he needed to buy a piece of his own property. It was Mr. Bates who convinced him to buy his lot in La Conchita, rather than continue to rent land from others."

Chet was also the one, along with Eleanor Gallardo, who was aware of the funding Bates was quietly providing to Punta Gorda School for supplies, special trips, parties, and most memorably an overnight field trip to the 1939 World's Fair in San Francisco. However, perhaps most significantly, on a personal level, Chet wrote the following about his brother Bobby: "When Bobby was born; he was born without a palate and would not be able to talk if it had not been for Mrs. Hughes and R.W. Bates who

Punta Gorda School field trip to the 1939 World's Fair, Treasure Island in San Francisco with support from Robert W. Bates. Pictured in front of the California Building from the left are Josie Dacayana, Mary Ruano, Francis Hughes, Edward Musick, Miss Davison, Shirley Dacayana, and Eleanor Gallardo. (*Eleanor Gallardo Ramey*)

arranged Bob's surgery at the Shrine hospital in San Francisco where a palate was grafted in his throat."[1]

The selected compositions are those that focus on Robert W. Bates' ongoing film projects at the Punta Gorda School, where the children were encouraged to dress in costumes and play act as part of their history and cultural studies lessons. Only a few minutes of film survives, but through the rich documentation of photos, oral histories, and actual student commentary and drawings from those years, we get a glimpse at just how much film has been lost. It is an amazing legacy of documentation testifying to Punta Gorda School's unique place in La Conchita history and in the history of public education in California. Of particular interest was R. W. Bates' dedication to multicultural education. He seemed to recognize how unique Punta Gorda School and La Conchita were as an integrated and truly multicultural learning environment and community.

Although people have found it surprising that such amazing academic accomplishments as the Punta Gorda School took place in La Conchita, they have all the hallmarks of this community's philosophy; most notable was the curriculum unheard of in most public schools until the 1960s-multicultural or cross-cultural education. Here was a one room school house where one teacher taught grades one through six with the most modest of resources. Yet it produced an extraordinary educational curriculum advanced for its time and unique in the educational system of this region.

Bessie Davison, the creative one-person force behind the whole educational program, was dearly loved by all of the students. Like Mary Poppins, little is known about her personal life in the over fourteen years she served as the only teacher at the Punta Gorda School. After the school closed, Miss Davison disappeared from California. There is no record or any commendations for her service in the Ventura County School Archives.

Robert W. Bates, Sr., *c.* 1930–40. (*Eleanor Gallardo Ramey*).

6

The Girls Who Lived in the School

The story I am about to relate has never been written before and parts of it may always remain a mystery since the story is based entirely on the memories of two young girls who were no doubt shielded from a great many details. The story is about Madeline Giles, who once was a successful and married hat designer in the Santa Barbara Riviera with her husband, Henry Giles; their son, Jack; and two younger daughters, Janet Elaine Giles and Mary Julanne Giles. The Giles had both become friends with Jim Slaybough, owner of the Thunderball Racetrack in Carpinteria, CA. All of the information I have comes from the memoires of one of their two daughters. At some point, Madeline started to have bouts of serious depression, which caused a serious strain on her marriage. Somehow, during one of their arguments, something was said that led Henry Giles to believe that Madeline's longtime friendship with Jim Slaybough was more than platonic and that he was not the real father of the girls. There is no proof that there was anything to this story. However, at that point, the family totally broke down. Madeline's husband left her and the two girls. This story was told to me by Mary Giles McDonough and cleared for publication. She wanted people to understand why her family was left in such a desperate situation. We chose not to go any further with that part of the story. Her brother, Jack, stayed mostly with his father and then with friends in La Conchita so he could finish high school at his school after his father moved away. When he came of age, he took a job with the railroad.

While the details were initially withheld from the girls, by the time they were through their elementary school years, with their father gone, they had lost their housing and just about everything else. They were destitute and somehow wound up living in the now-vacant Punta Gorda School. The Ventura school board made the decision to close the school in 1947 after the war. There were not enough children enrolled to keep the school open, but since it was a very sound building, it was useful for a number of organizations. This extraordinary school, which had a unique history, was about to end with a most dramatic closing. Both girls recognized for a long time that their mother had a delicate mental health stability. Today, she probably would be diagnosed with some form of bipolar depression.

So at their early ages, Janet and Mary really became part-time care givers. She had told them that their father had arranged for them to have this whole beautiful building to live in, but it was clear to the girls that they did not really have permission to live there. She told her daughters that when other people came into the building, they had to play a game of hide and be very quiet so the people who were there at choir practice or for some other rented occasion would not know they were in the building. "She thought we were really dumb. She had no idea we weren't babies anymore. She was just wrapped up in her own little world," Mary said.[1]

Mary believed that somehow her real father was involved in their living arrangements but was not sure. They did go to visit Jim Slaybaugh at his Thunderball farm in Carpinteria several times, but that certainly could have related to his longtime friendship with the Giles family.

On top of everything else, a cousin of Madeline's had deposited her daughter, Rosie, at the school for Madeline to take care of, too. Mary's mode of escape from this strange childhood was writing. Jan's was to fall in love at an early age, fortunately, with the right person, even though society was not ready for an interracial marriage in California in 1950, though that is the next story. For a researcher, one of the most interesting parts of this tale is Mary's documentation of the details we see of the Punta Gorda School. There is no other record of the building like this. The girls and their mother occupied the building for one year during 1948 and 1949. Mary Giles McDonough had handwritten commentary on the back side of each of these photos.

Janet and Mary Giles vamping on LC Beach, early 1946. (*Mary Giles McDonough*)

Punta Gorda School entrance, 1948. (*Mary Giles McDonough*)

View of school entrance Rd.
from La Conchita. School
actually was set in
Punta Gorda (a stop for
rail workers. The tree was
known to greyhound drivers
as "stop at the big tree"

Note on back of photo.

Above: Punta Gorda School front entrance as a home, 1948. (*Mary Giles McDonough*)

Left: Mary Giles as Annie Oakley in La Conchita, *c.* 1949. (*Mary Giles McDonough*)

Above left: Janet Elaine Giles in a coverall at Punta Gorda School front door, *c.* 1949. (*Mary Giles McDonough*)

Above right: Mary Giles and her dog, Feathers, on the front porch of Punta Gorda School, *c.* 1948–9. (*Mary Giles McDonough*)

My First Essay by Mary Julanne Giles McDonough

It seems only proper to write of the one person to influence me most and for the longest period of my life, my mother. My mother was a woman with many qualities, some good and yes, some bad. Yet her great qualities far out-weigh all the lesser ones. My mother gave me strength of character I have drawn upon innumerable times during my life. She also taught me to look for humor in all tribulations or true disasters. Such as when I was about ten, we somehow had gone from living on the Riviera in Santa Barbara to an abandoned school building on the Rincon, an area of coast between Ventura and Carpinteria. To think back now it must have been a terrible experience for her to face, alone with three small girls, yet for the three of us she made it and adventure. I adjusted well with her effervescent optimism.

As she arranged my room upon the stage at the far end of the building she bubbled on and on how not every girl had the opportunity to have a bedroom on a stage. She told me how I would be able to imagine myself to be anyone I wanted to be from my own mind or from the hundreds of books she had always made available to us.

> It was a great carefree life, though very poor, she would laugh and tell us "Just because you're poor you don't have to act poor." Little did we know that within a year we would be even poorer.
>
> The city decided to move the school building into town, using it as part of the Main firehouse. My mother protested loud and clear and when moving day came the workmen arrived to find my mother standing in the driveway with a gun. She simply refused to leave the property. The city did finally move the building but not my mother. She promptly set up house out in the open on top of the blacktop school ground. She made great fun out of marking off rooms, laying down rugs and setting all furniture in its place.
>
> Again I adjusted to this new living adventure, it was summer and still warm except for a little fog during the nights. At about this time the Ventura Welfare Dept. decided to rent us a house on the Avenue, not by any means the best section of the city. This move by the city gave me one of the most humorous memorable statements my mother was ever to leave me which has kept me laughing all these years.
>
> As the welfare people were happily telling her of their great gift of proper housing, she stood up, looked them straight in the eye and said, "no thank you, there was no way her girls were going to be raised on the wrong side of the tracks." I have laughed more thru the years, wrong side of the tracks? My god, we were living outside!
>
> She simply rose above it then and many more times during the years until she died. She taught me again and again any situation can be faced and overcome with a little bit of strength and a whole lot of humor.

The board and batten house was built by the "Gandy Dancers" on school property after the Punta Gorda School building was moved to Ventura. The Gandy Dancers were itinerant railroad workers, who Madeline Giles would invite to Sunday dinners during the months the family lived outside on the school playground. She would get out her best china, silverware, and set a formal dining table. The Gandy Dancers would often bring a chicken they cooked and they would all have dinner in grand style outside. It was to repay Madeline's kindness to them that these men built her the house after a flood from the canyon carried away the tent the family had erected during the winter rainy months.

My Retreat

The following is an excerpt by Mary Julanne (Giles) McDonough from 1982, published with permission of the author.

> I believe everyone should have a place to retreat for private contemplation. I have found a private place is necessary to keep body and soul—life itself—in balance. The retreat may be a real place to be alone or simply a private area within you mind where you may retreat to regain perspective.
>
> I was fortunate to discover my private hide-away many years ago as a young girl. My retreat was real. It was located high above the world on a special mountain, which rises above the sea north of Ventura, a small town found on the coast of California
>
> It was "somewhere" a young girl could find respite from the realities of life. This was a place to try to sort through a confused childhood. At these times, I found

Above left: Madeline Giles sitting in front of the board house built by the "Gandy Dancers" after the Punta Gorda School building was moved to Ventura, *c*. 1951. (*Mary Giles McDonough*)

Above right: Another view of Giles and the B&B house. (*Mary Giles McDonough*)

Right: Above La Conchita, 1971–2. (*Mary Giles McDonough*)

myself escaping more often to the top of the mountain, alone except for my constant companion, my dog Peggy Sue.

Peggy Sue and I would tramp upwards through the sage brush a trail overgrown, but not impassable. Finally when Peggy Sue and I would reach the top we would sit side by side and look out over the sea, breathing deeply the fresh wild perfume of sage.

For hours we would sit there taking it all in, a sea set against a backdrop of islands and pure blue sky. It was always a scene so beautiful I would immediately feel at peace inside and with this world that was around me. This place was so quiet I could hear my thoughts sort through all the turmoil held inside. Once in a while I would voice my thoughts out loud, breaking the silence. Peggy Sue would cock an eyebrow, look at me with her large questioning brown eyes and then snuggle in closer.

The two of us would stay there for hours, eventually the sun would start to slip into the ocean, signaling the end of the day. It was then that the fog would come rolling across the channel, like one never ending vision of cotton candy, tinted pink by the sinking sun and hiding everything it touched. I grew to love the fog, it's cool mist would descend around myself and Peggy Sue. It was as if this dense coolness added further protection from that outside world I knew I must return to.

Even now, as a woman of many years, I continue to return to this peaceful haven. I must admit however, I return less often in person, for "somehow the mountain seems so much higher to climb, then too, it's just not quite the same without my Peggy Sue beside me.

It's easier now to take my visits by way of "the mind". I can visualize each step climbing upwards, I can see myself reaching that special clearing at the top where once again I sit and turn my eyes and thoughts toward the sea. How marvelous is the mind, for my mind had captured the perfect photographs, filing each safely away somewhere within to be pulled at will to enjoy when needed? Through my minds' photo album I can return and picture the same vast ocean set against that familiar horizon of islands and blue, blue sky.

Once again I find a strength and calmness of spirit in returning, although it is now a place within myself, I still find the same peace needed to work through overwhelming problems. It was there that when my life looked dim, God gave me beauty. He gave me peace, strength, security, love and most of all the joy of spirit to survive.

Growing up in La Conchita by Chet Dacayana

The following was written in an email to the author on September 1, 2009.

In 1935 I moved to La Conchita from Carpinteria at early age of 5 with parents and older sister, Shirley. My parents purchased an old home on Zelzah Ave. where I grew up.

Dad worked on other farms in Carpinteria and on RW Bates Ranch before leasing land of his own and farming it. I enjoyed riding on the tractor while he disked the fields. Later on when I was old enough and could reach the brake and pedals, I was given that job, BOY I was in 7th heaven and felt like a big shot!!

We grew Lima and string beans, peas and tomatoes. It was a real challenge because there was no water available for irrigation. Water was not piped in until the mid-50s. Dad often took me crabbing, fishing and catching lobsters. Lobsters were so plentiful them days that when my dad would fish for perch, he would hook on to a lobster. He taught me to snorkel for lobsters by first tying a gunnysack on my belt, he then made a steel rod with a U-shaped end. The lobsters were normally half buried in the sand where they waited to pounce on a prey. He would pin them down with the U-shaped steel rod, grab them behind the head and quickly toss them in the gunnysack almost all in one motion!!! It took me a while to get the knack of it, but soon I got pretty good at it.

It was at the beach close to the Ventura–Santa Barbara County line where my dad stumbled onto some Indian artifacts. He uncovered a couple of stone bowls, pestles and then a large perfectly carved stone metate that I believe the Indians used to grind acorns. We rolled it on solid ground and with planks grunted it on my dad's model T Ford pick-up.

Because of working on my dad's farm, I was able to get a driver's license and work permit at the age of 14. So I was able to get a part time job after school, washing dishes and pots and pans at the Liberty Bells restaurant—I believe owned by Mr. Mears (don't remember his first name) He specialized in baked ribs and I was always covered with grease from head to toe!!!

At this restaurant is where I met EH Bates while he and his family were dining and I was helping clear tables (one of my times before I attacked the greasy pans in the kitchen) He asked if I would be interested in doing yard work. And that is how I got started working on his vast yard, apartment rentals and helping the carpenters, plumbers, and electricians.

We spent a lot of time on the beach before the freeway was built, our favorite hang-out was a small truck stop restaurant. The owner (boy, I can't think of her name) played honky-tonk music on that small piano of hers —she pounded the ivories like she was hammering nails—BIG NAILS!!! And her feet were stomping the foot pedals just as hard—it was GREAT!!!

During a winter storm along with gusts of wind and heavy seas, her old rickety pilings that held her building was pounded by giant waves until we could see that it was about to give way—a couple of us—Frank Hughes, Ted Gallardo, Mariano Razo and myself tried to rescue her beloved piano, but to no avail. It was heart-breaking to see that piano bobbing up and down on the giant waves.

When we weren't on the beach swimming, we were on our bikes. It was not unusual for a group of us to pedal to Carpinteria, get an ice cream cone then pedal back home. It was FUN TIME when it was grunion season. Got all the wood we could gather and build the biggest bon-fire that could be seen for miles. There we would B-B Q the grunions we caught and also some corn that we sort of borrowed from the near-by farm. One good thing--we didn't waste any!!!

In those days at times it was feast or famine. The famine was when our crops yield was not up to par and money was scarce. I can remember when my dad and I were in Carpinteria—I saw a boy with an ice-cream cone—I asked if I could have one—my dad with head down sadly said he didn't have any money. Another incident, when we were getting gas (on credit) at the corner Texaco station, Bill the proprietor was about to throw out some molding doughnuts my dad asked if he could have them—that was our dinner that evening, after we had removed all the mold off."

7

A La Conchita Love Story

In previous chapters, you were introduced to Chet Dacayana and Jan Giles. There were four years between them, which did not matter later, but when they first fell in love, it made it easier for authorities not to have to deal with the race card when Chet was sent to the work house and Jan (who was just underage and her home life admittedly was a shambles) was put into foster care. I will let Chet's narrative tell most of the story:

> As we grew up, Jan was sort of a Tom boy and wanted to hang out with us older guys—we constantly told her to GET LOST!!! But as the years rolled by I noticed her filling out, you might say, in the right places—truly I was getting attracted to her, but was too bashful and after all I was one of the guys that told her to get lost.
>
> One day while we were gathered on the beach, she came up to me and told me she was invited to a dance and was going with a boy from Carpinteria. She was concerned because she didn't know how to dance and asked if I knew how and if I did would I teach her. I said sure I'd be glad to (I myself couldn't dance, but thought, hey I could give it a try and bluff my way through). That evening she came over for the dance lesson—I gave her a feeble excuse that my mom wasn't feeling very good and didn't want to disturb her with loud music. She looked disappointed so I asked her if she would like to go to a football game in Carpinteria. Instead—she said GREAT let's Go—that was the beginning of our life together!! She did break her dance date!!
>
> We dated pretty steady after that. Because of our close relationship we were intimate and got in trouble with the authorities because of our age differences. Jan was placed in a foster home for 6 months. I spent the week-end in the County Facility and released due to the efforts of Margaret Hughes, and EH and RW Bates
>
> Having graduated from Ventura Jr. College, I proceeded on to Cal Poly College, at that time was located in San Dimas. I kept in touch with Jan through her mom. After that school term and Jan allowed to move back home so she could graduate with her Jr. High class, we plotted to elope in Tiana Mexico. Her mom, bless her soul, I'm sure

> knew of our plans. Jan made her reason for going with me to Cal Poly was to help pack up my belongings to come home for the summer. This happened on the summer of June 15, 1951.
>
> When we returned home and gave everyone the news, Jan's mom was ecstatic, but my mom said we were not married until we married in church. So Jan slept in my old bedroom and I slept in the front room couch until we were married a month later at the San Bueaventura Church in Ventura with our reception held at the Memorial Building in Carpinteria. The Filipino Community of Santa Barbara arranged the affair with a band, cake and a lot of food!!!
>
> Having a lot of out of town guests, and not able to afford a motel room, we spent our wedding night in the back seat of my '35 Ford.

Many people at the time thought this marriage would never last. She was only sixteen, from a dysfunctional family situation, old beyond her years, and did not even have a high school degree. He was a poor member of a minority race, who just married an attractive white woman early in the 1950s when such things were barely tolerated and often brought out extreme hostility in some people. As I began to review this material once more, my fervent wish was that some of those naysayers lived long enough to learn of Chet and Jan's triumphs and awards for their work with youths over the fifty years

Chet on the beach, early 1950s. (*Bill Mingus*)

Janet and Mary Giles on La Conchita Beach, *c.* 1951. (*Mary Giles McDonough*)

Janet (left) and Mary Giles (far right) and friends in La Conchita, *c.* 1950–1. (*Mary Giles McDonough*)

Above left: Chet Dacayana's graduation picture, 1950.

Above right: A formal portrait of Janet Elaine Giles, 1950. (*Mary Giles McDonough*)

Right: The wedding of Chester (Chet) Dacayana and Janet Giles, Old Mission Church, Ventura in 1951. (*Chet Dacayana*)

Above: The wedding reception of Chet Dacayana and Janet Giles.

Left: Janet and Chet Dacayana with their children, Lalana and Jana, late 1950s. (*Chet Dacayana*)

of their marriage. It was not about being smug or proving them wrong so much as to get people to think about people and places beyond the superficial or making immediate judgements. Jan not only finished high school but continued her education and earned a college degree in education and psychological counseling, serving as superintendent of the youth building at the Ventura County Fair for thirty-seven years and receiving the Ojai Woman of the Year award for her work with the Humane Society and senior citizens.

Chet was inducted into the Ventura County Sports Hall of Fame for serving as a baseball and football umpire in both high school and college games for over twenty-five years. They had two children, adopted three more, and in their over fifty years together took in over 100 foster children, many coming from severely abused situations. They were treated to a gala fiftieth wedding celebration in 2001. Both of them are gone now, but they had a beautiful life together.

Aunt Mary Giles (McDonough) with nieces Lalana (left) and Jana (right) above La Conchita Beach in 1959. (*Mary Giles McDonough*)

8

The La Conchita Gang

A highly unusual and poignant photo story was taken by a number of different members of the "La Conchita Gang," as they were called. They did not think of themselves as a gang, but others outside La Conchita did. They were just a group of close friends, but in the early 1950s, this area was not accustomed to seeing a group of mixed-race teenage boys who hung out together and all tried to look like James Dean. The camera was a gift from someone; a friend named Teresa gave them an album in 1954 to put all the photos in. Not all of the fifty-five photos are good, but some are wonderful. Bill Mingus, one of the group, wrote a great commentary on the photos. Allen Blackwell gave me the photo album and an interview before he passed away.

Growing up in La Conchita

by Bill Mingus

We moved from Richmond California to La Conchita in the summer of 1948. While on vacation from Richmond, we stopped at a small gas station on the beach across from La Conchita. Based upon what the station owners told my parents they bought several lots. I still remember clearing one of them enough for me to Dad to erect a surplus Army tent that was our home for a year or two. I started the 4th grade in September of 48. I was in La Conchita until July of 1956 when I joined the Navy for four years, school and I just didn't get along well.

La Conchita was a great place to grow up. I have many good memories of those years. I remember learning to swim in the ocean, but the first time I got brave enough to swim out beyond large breakers to the Kelp beds I got creamed coming back through those waves. I thought I was in a washing machine, bouncing off the bottom, getting to the surface only to be pulled back into the sand again and again. I thought I was going to drown ... but I didn't.

I remember fires on the beach during the day when we would place a wire screen over the fire, then dig clams, and toss them near the fire. The guys near the fire would

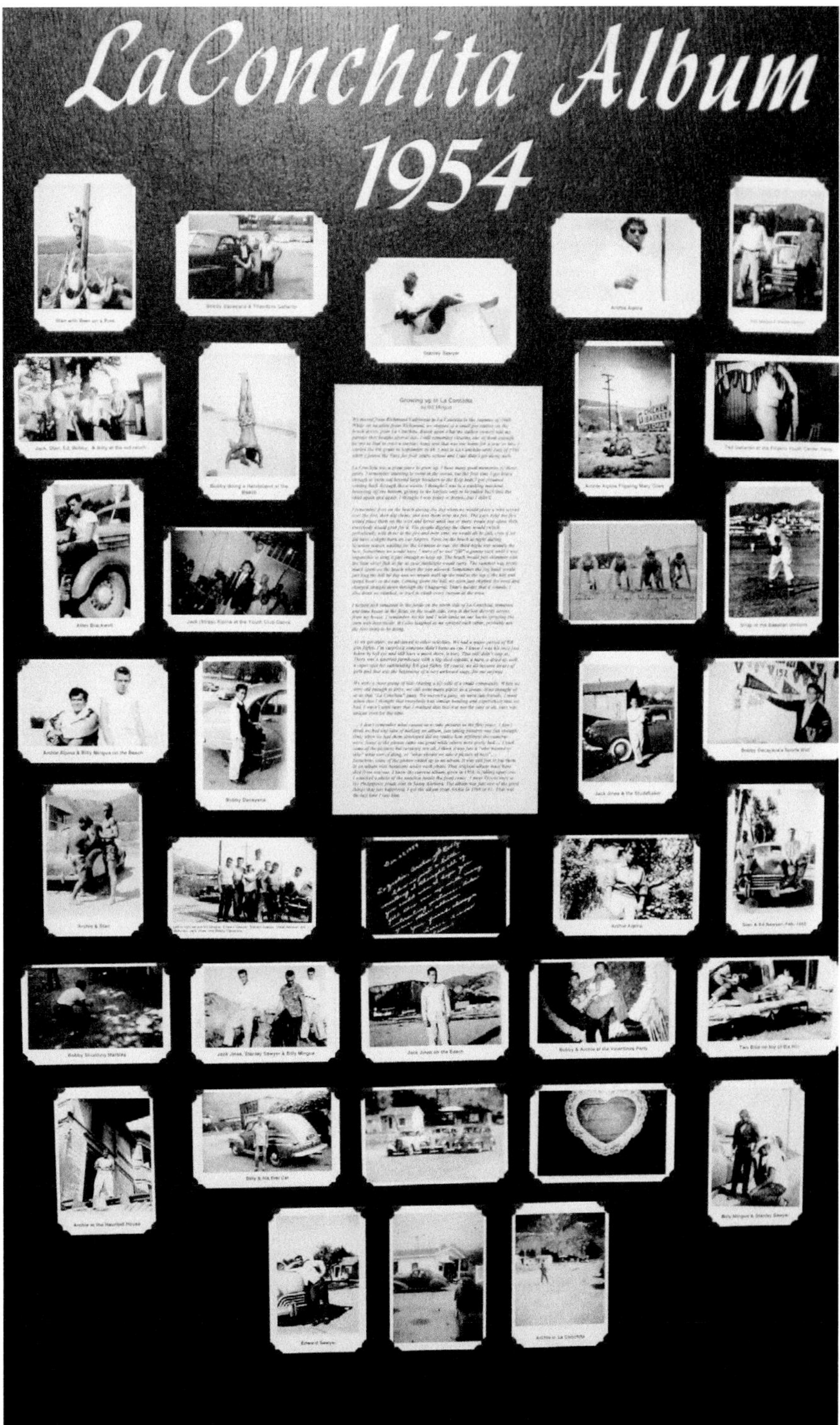

Photobook installation from 2010 exhibition.

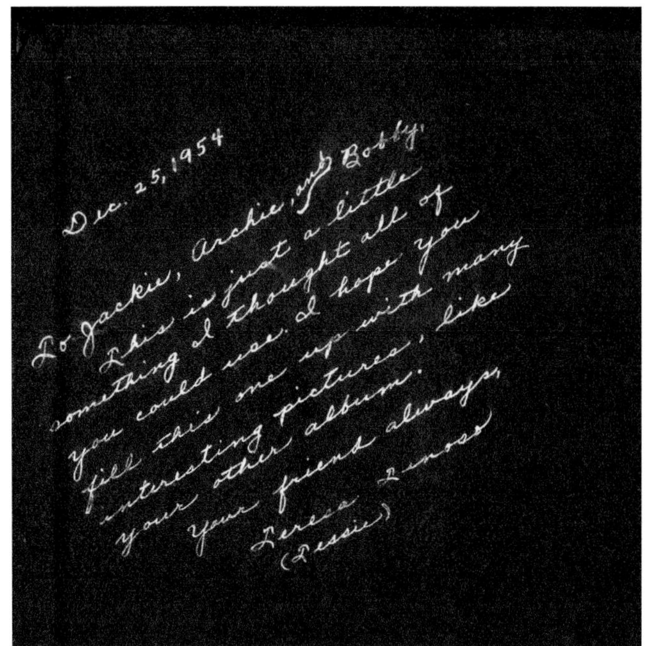
Dec. 25, 1954
To Jackie, Archie, and Bobby,
This is just a little
something I thought all of
you could use. I hope you
fill this one up with many
interesting pictures, like
your other album.
Your friend always,
Teresa Tinoso
(Tessie)

Left: Teresa's photograph scrapbook with photos, 1954.

Below: The gang's all here.

Just like James Dean.

Tough guys.

place them on the wire and hover until one or more would pop open, then everybody would grab for it. The people digging the clams would switch periodically with those at the fire and over time, we would all be full, even if we did have a slight burn on our fingers. Fires on the beach at night during Grunion season waiting for the Grunion to run, the third night was usually the best. Sometimes we would have 7 more of us and "fill" a gunny sack until it was impossible to drag it fast enough to keep up. The beach would just shimmer with the little silver fish as far as your flashlight would carry. The summer was pretty much spent on the beach when the sun allowed. Sometimes the fog bank would just hug the hill all day and we would walk up the road to the top if the hill and spend hours in the sun. Coming down the hill, we often just skipped the road and charged straight down through the Chaparral. That's harder that it sounds. I also think we climbed, or tried to climb every canyon in the area.

I helped pick tomatoes in the fields on the north side of La Conchita, tomatoes and lima beans in the fields on the south side, corn in the lots directly across from my house. I remember Archie and I with tanks on our backs spraying the corn with insecticide. We also laughed as we sprayed each other, probably not the best thing to be doing.

As we got older, we advanced to other activities. We had a major period of BB gun fights. I'm surprised someone didn't lose an eye. I know I was hit once just below by left eye and still have a mark there, it hurt. That still didn't stop us. There was a deserted farmhouse with a big shed outside, a barn, a dried up well, a super spot for outstanding BB gun fights. Of course, we all became aware of girls and that was the beginning of a very awkward stage, for me anyway.

We were a close group of kids sharing a life style of a small community. When we were old enough to drive, we still went many places as a group. Most thought of us as that "La Conchita" gang. We weren't a gang, we were just friends. I must admit that I thought that everybody had similar bonding and experiences that we had. I wasn't until later that I realized that that was not the case at all, ours was unique even for the time.

... I don't remember what caused us to take pictures in the first place. I don't think we had any idea of making an album, just taking pictures was fun enough. Only when we had them developed did we realize how different the cameras were. Some of the photos came out great while others were pretty bad.... I took some of the pictures but certainly not all. I think it was just a "who wanted to take" what sort of thing, or "what should we take a picture of next" ... Somehow, some of the photos ended up in an album. It was still fun to put them in an album with notations under each photo. That original album must have died from overuse. I know the current album, given in 1954, is falling apart too. I attached a photo of the notation inside the front cover. I met Teresa once at the Philippines youth club in Santa Barbara. The album was just one of the good things that happened. I got the album from Archie in 1960 or 61. That was the last time I saw him.

9

Highway Widening and Finding Charlie Chan's Cottage

Losing Half of Paradise

In 1949, the highway was widened to four lanes, marking the separation of La Conchita from its beloved seashore. During the widening of the highway, most of the cottages on the beach at La Conchita and Mussel Rock (Mussel Shoals) were either forced to move to a new location or were demolished. A few of the cottages from the beach were moved to La Conchita. Some of them were moved to Rincon Point and others to Sea Cliff Colony.

They were protected by a riprap seawall of boulders weighing up to 10 tons brought by rail from Riverside County. This monumental rock wall combined with the timber trestle pier built by the oil company at Mussel Shoals in order to drill ocean wells, caused the entrapment of sand and the buildup of beach in front of the sea wall and reduced the intensity of wave action. While this made it possible for the division of highways to work out a more economical way of widening the highway, locals complained bitterly that this construction had dramatically changed the natural shoreline. It destroyed the habitat for local lobsters and other shellfish, which previously had been abundantly available just offshore.

The widening of the highway also marked the separation of La Conchita from its beloved seashore. During the widening of the highway, most of the cottages on the beach at La Conchita and Mussel Rock (Mussel Shoals) were either forced to move to a new location or were demolished. A few of the cottages from the beach were moved to La Conchita. Some of them were moved to Rincon Point and others to Sea Cliff Colony.

It was devastating to this little community to lose its access to its heart—the beach, the shore, and the sea. It was not just for entertainment; for this poor community, it was sustenance too. Before the rock wall came in, a boat was not even needed as shell fish were plentiful. During the right months, mussels, clams, and crabs were abundant. Much of that changed with the rock wall and its action in tandom with the rock jetty

Above: Aerial view of La Conchita with some houses still being moved from the beach, 1950. (*Ray Blackwell*)

Left: Jack Jines on La Conchita Beach with a few cottages still there. (*Bill Mingus*)

Ray Blackwell, remembering the story.

built by the oil company. Together, they had a major effect on wave movement in the bay. With the highway and only little narrow access to the beach, there was no way to get even a small boat out to fish either.

Promises were made from the very beginning to include beach access for La Conchita as budget line items in any subsequent highway projects, and there were certainly going to be a number of them. Highway projects came and went; one or two included vague language about beach access but ran out of funding before it could even be debated. Then came the big widening project of 1972; somebody actually included "the La Conchita Underpass" as a line item on the program for the widening project. I came upon this interesting document while doing research for this book and started asking questions about whether there were funds actually allocated for the project and why nothing ever happened.

However, this was losing focus on my task at hand. I was interested in knowing where all those houses on the beach went. Some that were just summer bungalows were destroyed. Many were moved, and it was very interesting where they landed. Keeping in mind that from the very beginning, once local realtors and investors realized who they had let get established on the Gold Coast, a large group of financially oriented people from our area had been trying to fix this mistake. So it seems especially ironic that a goodly number of these La Conchita beach homes would wind up in the exclusive gated community of Rincon Point. Here, they are considered vintage, rare, and antique. Some were also moved to Mussel Shoals among the mega mansions. I was interested in finding someone that had actually had a house on the beach and moved it. La Conchita may only be ten blocks long, but every time I have wished for something, somebody here has it or can help me; it is pretty amazing. The house in question is on the next block and belonged to Allen Blackwell. He has passed away but was one of my La Conchita Elders. His brother, Ray Blackwell, filled in the story of the move from the beach.

Left: From the left: Allen Blackwell, girl with dog, and Ray Blackwell by their beach house on La Conchita Beach, upper left, *c*. 1944. (*Ray Blackwell*)

Below: The Blackwell house shortly after it was moved across the railroad tracks to Santa Paula Avenue, *c*. 1944. (*Ray Blackwell*)

The Blackwell house on Santa Paula Ave, as it looks today. (*Author's collection*)

> The first picture was taken about 1944. My brother Allen is on the left, I do not remember who the girl is, I am on the right. Our house is the upper left corner. It belonged to Mrs. Parsons. My Dad worked for her at the Parsons Ranch. The freeway was coming through that part of the beach and the house was sold for $50 I believe. My Dad bought it and had it moved to La Conchita for $500. The lot he placed it on he bought from Mr. Borman for $100 in about 1944. You can check with my brother Allen, he seems to have a better memory of these events than I do but I am close.

Update: Getting Paradise Back

Three years ago, Ventura County finally made good on the promise it made to the La Conchita over sixty years ago when it first widened the highway and cutting the beach portion of the community off and not providing any safe access to it. The promise was to provide a passageway during the next widening project, though there were several widening projects. The La Conchita passageway was to be a part of at least one of them, but funding for it was not there when it was needed. While I was doing my research, I came across a program for the 1972 ribbon cutting of the new highway project, which listed "the La Conchita Underpass" as one of the projects to be funded then. What happened? What happened to the money allocated for it? Armed with a written document and apparently an allotted budget that had somehow disappeared, the La Conchita Community Organization (LCCO) established a dialogue with State Government officials. I had found a document that was thirty-five years old, it only took another decade to bring about a resolution. Now we finally have this beautiful 8-foot high passageway with a bikeway above, more people are venturing into our little paradise and falling in love with another La Conchita hidden jewel. Not only do we have a beautiful pristine beach but the beach sits at the edge of a federally protected Marine Mammal Sanctuary, where dolphin and harbor seals can be regularly viewed. It is also within viewing and biking distance to Rincon Point and its famous Surfing Classic.

Curator's Commentary: Serendipity: In Search of Charlie Chan's Cottage

I had searched for the whereabouts of this cottage for over two years. All the other cottages had either been moved to either Mussel Rock or La Conchita, or were destroyed. I would learn later that off the record a few others had crossed the County Line, but I had given up. There is a saying I coined especially for La Conchita while doing this research, "IF YOU CAN'T FIND WHAT YOU ARE LOOKING FOR, ITS TIME TO STOP LOOKING & IT WILL FIND YOU!" So it happened just like that. My husband, Bill, was a docent at a nearby botanical gardens. A field trip was planned to the gardens of a cottage on Rincon Point. Docents were able to invite their spouses to join them on the trip. As we approached the Lindley Cottage, there was something that seemed familiar about it. Even before I entered that front door and saw the large movie poster, I knew where I was and that it had found me.

I find it ironic that a cottage from La Conchita Beach considered lower class by most of its neighbors escapes destruction and winds up in a gated community on the classiest point on the Gold Coast and is now considered vintage, rare, and rented for a premium amount as a posh guest house—it is all in the celebrity label.

Warner Oland owned a cottage on the beach between La Conchita and Mussel Rock. For those very young or not at all into popular old movies, the Swedish-born Warner Oland was a veteran stage actor with numerous film credits, who will always be best remembered as the first actor to breathe life into an incredibly popular movie character named Charlie Chan. He played the inscrutable detective in some sixteen movies. However, his first debut as a faux Asian was to play the Mysterious Dr. Fu Manchu in the 1929 film of the same name. He was also the first actor to portray a werewolf in a major Hollywood film, *The Werewolf of London* in 1935. Yet it was as a result of being cast as the international detective Charlie Chan opposite Marlene Dietrich and Anna May Wong in the classic film *Shanghai Express* (1932), which made worldwide success for him and the Charlie Chan character and led to tremendous box office success and sixteen films. Oland married Edith Gardener Shearn, well-known at that time as a playwright and accomplished portrait painter.

Movie poster of Warner Oland as Charlie Chan, the most famous La Conchita/Mussel Rock area cottage owner to have his abode removed from the beach, *c.* 1940s. (*The Carr Gallery*)

The "Oland Cottage" as it appears today on Rincon Point, where it was moved from the La Conchita area beachfront in the mid- to late 1940s. (*The Lindley Institute*)

Above left: Interior of Oland Cottage today, with few changes from the original structure. (*The Lindley Institute*)

Above right: A section of an original delicately painted mural by Oland's wife, Edith Gardener Shearn, is still in its original setting in Oland Cottage, *c.* 1940. (*The Lindley Institute*)

10

Local Heroes and Famous People

Magdalena Razo

Magdalena Razo was a legend when her life was celebrated in the *Ventura Star Press* in 1999, and it was quite a life. She was a survivor of the Mexican Revolution at four. A La Conchita Elder, she moved to this tiny enclave in 1938. She married an Indian shaman, and she and her husband were among the founding families of La Conchita, where she happily lived for over sixty years, until she died in 2007 at 103. Many of her children and grandchildren added to the population of La Conchita.

Tony Alvis

The 2005 La Conchita mudslide took the life of one of the community's unique individuals. Tony Alvis was the founder of the Los Padres Wilderness Outfitters, the mountain guide service that enabled visitors to experience the Sespe Wilderness back country of the Los Padres National Forest in all its world beauty on horseback. This mountain guide service takes visitors into one of the most scenic areas of old California, leaving it unspoiled and experiencing it as it existed before the advent of modern travel. The Sespe is a fitting legacy to the life he loved and introduced to so many.

Linda Merrill

Linda Merrill is the woman who broke through the glass ceiling for women in surfing. Merrill became famous for her tandem surfing talent and surfboard ballet. She is a notable figure as she was the first woman to have her picture on the cover of a major surfing magazine. The following pages show her in all her glory.

A SURF PAS DE DEUX

LEGENDARY SURF GIRL [illegible] LOOKS BACK

by RUSS SPENCER

Above: Magdalena Razo was a legend just by her very presence. A La Conchita Elder, she moved to this tiny enclave in 1938 but lived more life than most of us ever will. She survived the Mexican Revolution at the age of four; she then married an Indian shaman and lived to the age of 103. (*Ventura County Star*)

Left: "A Surf Pas De Deux: Legendary Surf Girl Linda Merrill Looks Back," *Santa Barbara Magazine*, Nov./Dec. 2005.

Right: Cover of *Surfer Magazine* (international surfing magazine), November 1964.

Below: Surfing photo of Linda Merrill by John Fowler, 1962, San Clemente CA. Recognized as one of the premier early women surfers, she traveled the world during the 1960s with male surfers who later became surfing legends, including Duke Kahanamoku (the Father of Surfing). Merrill moved to La Conchita in the 1990s.

Huntington Beach U.S. Surfboard Championships Official Program, September 1967. The program costs 25 cents. (*Linda Merrill cover*)

Tony Alvis (1951–2005) with his horse, Mutah, and his dog, Tabasco. The 2005 La Conchita mudslide took the life of one of the community's unique individuals. Tony Alvis was the founder of the Los Padres Wilderness Outfitters, the mountain guide service that enabled visitors to experience the Sespe Wilderness back country of the Los Padres National Forest in all its unspoiled beauty. The Sespe is a fitting legacy to the life he loved and introduced to so many. (*Los Padres Wilderness Outfitters and the Alvis family*)

Seaside Banana Gardens Park, *c.* early 1990s. (*Rob Freeman*)

Seaside Banana Gardens Park sign. (*Rob Freeman*)

Plantation bosses Doug Richardson, right, and Paul Turner are split by a banana-coiffed model in the guise of Carmen Miranda.

SUCCESS COMES IN BUNCHES FOR TWO CALIFORNIANS, PURVEYORS OF BANANAS BORN—AND GROWN—IN THE U.S.A.

Military coups pose no threat to their colorful domain, populated by Blue Ja-yas, Jamaican Reds and orange-yel-

cut, Vermont, Massachusetts, New Jersey—all over the East," he says proudly.

old lemons and limes, he decided to t out some tropical plants purely for their ornamental qualities. Since ev-

People Magazine, August 8, 1988, p. 82.

The popular La Conchita roadside attraction was one of the few banana plantations in North America.

S.B. News-Press 2-8-98

Photography by Steve Malone, News-Press

BANANA grower splits

By BARRY BORTNICK
NEWS-PRESS STAFF WRITER

La Conchita's Seaside Banana Garden will be bulldozed this month, ending a 13-year experiment in exotic agriculture and eliminating one of the South Coast's most beloved roadside attractions.

Nearly 100,000

Santa Barbara News-Press, 1998.

Seaside Banana Gardens: Doug Richardson and Paul Turner

For thirteen years, Seaside Banana Gardens Park attracted worldwide attention and media attention (even controversy) from the late 1970s to the mid-1990s. *People* magazine did a spread on Seaside Banana Gardens. There were articles in leading newspapers from the *Chicago Tribune* to the *LA Times* on Doug Richardson and his partner, Paul Turner, growing more than fifty-five varieties of bananas—most of them tropical varieties horticulturists insisted could not grow in California's climate; however, they did not know about La Conchita's magical microclimate. Private subscription botanical magazines and journals followed suit with articles. The Banana Gardens became a favorite stop on highway 101 until 1995, when they lost their lease.

The Seaside Banana Gardens operated by Doug Richardson and Paul Turner was the most famous attraction in La Conchita from its opening in 1985 until it closed in 1996. The Gardens were featured in national and international publications and made La Conchita a destination along Highway 101. While horticultural authorities maintained that bananas could not be commercially grown in California, Richardson and Turner proved them wrong by cultivating over fifty exotic varieties. La Conchita's unique microclimate was ideal for this purpose.

A Banana Fable

Even though the Seaside Banana Gardens packed up and left La Conchita over twenty-six years ago, banana plants still pop up wherever they can in our yards (as seen on the opposite page). "Why are you still here?" I asked one volunteer about to take over my yard. "I'm seeking asylum," I distinctly heard the banana answer. "We heard La Conchita people were fun and liked surprises." "We do," I replied, "but it depends on how much space you take up and your blossoms drool sticky stuff all over the place." "Hey, you live in La Conchita, you know there is always a little bad with the good. We left the plantation, we are free, people in La Conchita of all places should welcome us and give us sanctuary! We're not going back. We like it here. It's the best place for a healthy banana plant to be. Be generous, quite griping and just eat the bananas!"

Banana plants escape the plantation and seek asylum in La Conchita. This 12-foot banana plant resided in my garden until we had to cut it down for reaching over the wall of our property and letting its blossom drool on my neighbor's truck. (*Author's collection*)

11

Roger Brown and La Conchita:
Made for Each Other

If ever an artist and a place were made for each other, there was no greater match in American art than Roger Brown and La Conchita. The artist was checking out properties in California, looking for a warm place for a new home. Landing in La Conchita had more to do with his impulsive collecting nature than any other factor. Roger Brown fell in love with the Spartan "Royal Mansion" trailer that was the only residence on the property at 6754 Ojai Avenue in La Conchita when he purchased it in 1988. These luxurious aircraft trailers were made by the J. Paul Getty Construction Co. and mass produced between 1946 and 1962. The exceptional details on the hand -crafted wood interiors and other little extras made these trailers very enticing to a collecting fanatic like Roger Brown. Now that the artist had his collectable dream playhouse, he knew what else he needed: "A Temple of Painting," as he would call it.

Brown hired internationally known architect Stanley Tigerman to design his studio and living space; he then fought for over two years to get the design of this studio through the Ventura County Planning Commission. He commemorated his frustrations with the commission in a famous painting entitled *Citizens Killing Themselves After Dealing with the Ventura County Planning Commission*. In the artist's 1988–1989 sketchbook, the title of the painting is given a subtitle that is in part a quotation from 1979 hit song "All the Gold in California" by Larry Gatlin and the Gatlin Brothers; Brown writes: "If you're dreaming of California it doesn't matter where you played before California is a whole new game."

A number of La Conchitans can relate to the artist's frustration. Residents have been issued citations for simple or creative enhancements to their homes for no particular reasons that make any sense. People can understand the county's concern over additions that might pose a potential threat to health, safety, or other potential liabilities, but they have also been issued citations for things like simple carports, roof gardens, and front yard flower gardens, which were a tad beyond some invisible line over a non-existent sidewalk and ordered to be destroyed or removed by the violation deadline or face a daily heavy fine.

Right: Stanley Tigerman / Tigerman McCurry, drawing of the Roger Brown Studio. *Circa* 1990.

Below: Roger Brown (1941–1997) *Citizens Killing Themselves After Having To Deal With the Ventura County Coastal Planning Commission (if you're dreaming of California it doesn't matter where you played before California is a whole new game)*, 1989 oil on canvas, 48 x 72 in. Courtesy of the School of the Art Institute of Chicago and Kavi Gupta. Photo: William H. Bengtson.

Left: Roger Brown and his dog Elvis at the Spartan Royal Mansion trailer. Photographer and date unknown. (*Courtesy of the Roger Brown Study Collection, the School of Art Institute of Chicago*)

Below: Architectural rendering of the Brown Studio/Residence, *c.* 1989. (*Courtesy of the Roger Brown Study Collection, the School of Art Institute of Chicago*)

Above left: Roger Brown in his La Conchita studio with the painting *Rosa Foetida Bicolor* in progress, *c.* 1994, photographer unknown.

Above right: *Roger Brown: Calif: U.S.A.*, exhibition catalogue cover. (*SAIC/Roger Brown Estate*)

Right: Roger Brown home/studio and Spartan trailer at 6754 Ojai, La Conchita, CA.

Roger Brown (1941–1997), *Calif. U.S.A. With Astonished Couple*, 1995, oil on canvas, wood, ceramic objects, 48 × 60 × 12 in. Courtesy of the School of the Art Institute of Chicago and Kavi Gupta. Photo: William H. Bengtson.

For a time, Ventura County Government was outwardly negative toward La Conchita and its residents. Unfortunately, Brown's design for his residence hit the Planning Committee during this rather nasty period. This hostility was just an extension of the kind of activity originally faced by the La Conchita Elders once it was apparent that this community was going to be successful and people had no intention of leaving. For the county, it was the matter of the present limited tax base on the last piece of ideally situated property on the Gold Coast of CA with its coveted microclimate and the most direct access to the pristine beach. The county had been trying to correct a momentary mistake made ninety-five years ago that let the "wrong kinds of people build a community in La Conchita." As late as 1995, when I called the county clerk's office for some information, the clerk I reached told me I was stupid for living in La Conchita and hung up.

In studying this situation, I concluded some time ago that the difficulty encountered by Brown in getting Tigerman's design approved by the Ventura Planning Commission and the negativity experienced by people in La Conchita were based on the same thing: "Fear," namely fear of difference and that it will spread if not checked; fear of the "Other;" fear and resentment of people living an alternate lifestyle (people living by standards that they do not understand); fear of people not entitled to live in the area that they are living in; or fear of people "who color outside the lines."

The dominant majority may have no idea what it is that they fear; they do not have to know as they are in charge and like things the way they are. Many years ago, I took part in an NEH seminar, and the most memorable moments of the discussion that made a lasting impression on me I see everywhere in my research now was a presentation by cultural anthropologist Virginia Dominguez, which discussed all the implications of entitlement in societies on both the conscious and subconscious levels.

Strangely enough, it was a sympathetic governor after the 2005 mudslide that started to change Ventura County's point of view. A few other things happened to turn the tide and forced the county to become more user-friendly to La Conchita, back off on citations, and follow through on many promises to this community. The most relevant one to this book has been an awareness of Roger Brown's painting, *Citizens Killing Themselves After Dealing with the Ventura County Planning Commission.* Although the painting was not featured in the 2010 exhibition at the Carpinteria, it was referred to in the educational materials and also on tours to view the house in La Conchita. After the exhibition was featured on the front page of the *Ventura County Star*, more people became aware of the painting and that it certainly did not show county government in a good light. It would definitely go on to be seen nationally at some point. As long as Roger Brown remained an internationally known artist, while getting comical responses, this painting would stand as a condemnation for the kind of inept bureaucratic committee process that drives people crazy. Bowing to the power of art and a number of another factors, Ventura County definitely changed its attitude towards La Conchita.

Unfortunately, almost 100 years of negativity passed around and magnified by long time elite members of the Santa Barbara community and the media cannot be easily washed away. We belong to many cultural organizations and still when I say I live in La Conchita, I get that look of tightened lips and shake of the head, but this does not happen nearly as much as it once did. If I am in my New York fighting mode, I will engage by asking if they have actually ever spent any time in La Conchita. That produces very frightened responses. My victim's eyes start darting around the room, looking for an escape route. I really have to stop doing this as it is not good diplomacy for the cause.

Roger Brown must have felt very comfortable in his new environment (aside from Ventura County's bureaucracy) since he shared with his new La Conchita neighbors a predilection for obsessive, eclectic collecting of all manner of things from the divine to the quirky and almost everything curious in between. That sounds so familiar to most people living in La Conchita. It takes either an experienced artist or a resident dreamer to see things that have yet to "become" something, or are in the process of emerging. All over La Conchita, you can see things dragged back from the beach, machine parts, slump glass, and parts of antique chairs fulfilling their Karma and going on to their next lives in people's yards, open garages, and porches.

The artist's new "Temple of Painting," as he referred to his new studio, also had plenty of room for all of the many things he collected. He would joyfully go on collecting trips for ceramics with his good friend, Linda Cathcart. Cathcart directed Casa Delores (the

Museum of Mexican Folk Art) until her death in 2018. However, he would also pick up things in flea markets, garage sales, or view flyers. For Brown, there was a great democracy in things:

> Brown saw beauty in the detail of all these things placing them in his collection alongside art works by his contemporaries The deliberate placing and arrangement of high art with low vernacular objects was connected for Brown to an impulse to value the evidence of human creativity and the endeavor that it represents whenever he saw it.[1]

In La Conchita, it seems everyone collects. From the offerings that the sea leaves for us on our beach to the special finds from our travels, to things we pick up and for some unknown reason we cannot live without, collecting fills us with a sense of purpose. Every year, we have a community -wide garage sale, and while I have not done an official count, it seems to me that almost half the community buys the treasures the other half is selling. We, too, are a community that sees beauty and possibilities in all things.

Brown was a hopelessly eclectic collector of things—some valuable and vintage, other items that one would consider junk; however, to Brown, who elevates old irons to modernist-era armed cars and sees other possibilities in such things, everything has value. Everything is designed by somebody at some point and has a spirit looking for a connection. Everything has value in its own way; it just depends on your perspective. He enshrines them all and elevates even the ugliest or lowliest of objects so that we might really look at it for the first time; perhaps it would be best to say that we might really "see" it for the first time.

I believe the artist came under the spell of La Conchita. Everything about this quirky little place enforced his eclectic ideas about high and low art. There was something else that happened, too. He loved plants; that was one of the reasons he wanted to move somewhere warm. It was here where he saw the magic of La Conchita's microclimate making trees out of house plants as if one of his surreal paintings had come to life. I have never undertaken a complete inventory of Brown's paintings and mixed media works, so I do not know for sure when he started doing tiny human figures and colossal flora. If he started that theme prior to coming to La Conchita, he must have thought he drifted into one of his own dreams. If this was a new theme actually presenting itself to him, it must have seemed as if he had walked into an inspiration in his own mind. The microclimate here is more than amazing, it is magic. We say that if you have a dying house plant, stick it in La Conchita's soil and watch it revive. What we do not tell you (because we do not want to scare people) is that if it is a Schefflera, Bird of Paradise, Hibiscus, or any other moderately sized common house or patio plant, within a relatively short time, it will grow into a monster. Outside my front window is a two-story 'Bird of Paradise' and across the street, I look out every day at a 35-foot Schefflera. The quick, lush growth of plants here is astounding—even plants that are true topicals and are not supposed to grow in south central California. That the artist paid homage to this phenomenon is not surprising.

The La Conchita community and its environment inspired many of Roger Brown's paintings during the last decade of his life. The Virtual Still Lifes the artist created with ceramic pottery he collected while living in La Conchita are now considered an

Above left: Roger Brown (1941–1997), *Rosa Foetida Bicolor*, 1994, oil on canvas, 48 × 72 in. Courtesy of the School of the Art Institute of Chicago and Kavi Gupta. Photo: William H. Bengtson.

Above right: Roger Brown (1941–1997) *Bonsai #5, Literati (Bunjing)*, 1997, oil on canvas, 72 × 48 in. Courtesy of the School of the Art Institute of Chicago and Kavi Gupta. Photo: William H. Bengtson.

Virtual Still Life #15 Waterfalls and Pitchers (1995). Oil on canvas, mixed media, 37 1/2 × 50 × 9 inches (95.3 × 127 × 22.9 cm). Collection of the Flint Institute of Arts, Flint, MI. (*Roger Brown Study Collection, The School of the Art Institute of Chicago*)

significant period of work in his career. A selected group of these paintings were the subject of a major exhibition, which opened in Chicago in June (and continued through October) 2010 at the Hyde Park Art Center—*Roger Brown: Calif. U.S.A.*

By coincidence, that show in Chicago opened at the same time the 2010 "La Conchita: Reclaiming Its History" exhibition opened in Carpinteria, CA. La Conchita was pleased to have contributed some curatorial assistance and hospitality support for the development of that Chicago exhibition. Twenty-two years after the artist's death, critical interest in Brown's La Conchita paintings has grown. In May 2019, "Roger Brown: Virtual Still Lifes" (the artist's first major solo museum exhibition) opened at the Museum of Art and Design (MAD) in New York, and there is more to come.

I have thought a lot about why this body of work and related pieces have captured critical attention. It is because somehow Brown has managed to imbue them with a bit of La Conchita magic. They "become more than the sum of their parts"—become, or rather "becoming," is the key word. "Emergent" and "transformational" are also key words or concepts. Viewed from a different perspective, "virtual" is a theme that can easily be seen and felt. These are objects caught in their moment of transition, or wished for transformation. The excitement is all about the state of becoming. La Conchita, its microclimate, and its dreamers, inventors, collectors, poets, gardeners, and artists are all about the moment of transformation. Is there anything more exciting than that? The Virtual Still Lifes perform this emergence or transformation tongue in cheek, but that is acceptable here. This is just my theory based on a number of things I have seen among the artist's collectables. Perhaps the last chapter of this book will convince you of its merit.

Tiny La Conchita is proud to have played a part in the artist's creative production in the last years of an astounding career. Roger Brown's pink adobe home and studio is the major landmark of La Conchita, CA.

The exhibition was organized by the Roger Brown Study Collection at the School of Art Institute of Chicago. The La Conchita site and its Roger Brown's Studio Residence played an important role in the presentation of this exhibition.

12

An Angel and A Hero Once Lived Next Door

John Beck, Anti-Hero

The fact that La Conchita was saved from the flames of the Thomas Fire—at that time, the largest fire in California's history, when all around it every community and forest area had burned—made national news. None of the news vehicles mentioned the real reason we were spared, but everyone in our little pocket of the mountainside knew why.

Setting the Record Straight

In the wee small hours of the morning of December 6, 2017, I had one of the most harrowing experiences of my life. The Thomas Fire had been making its way toward La Conchita for most of the day, moving slowly since the Santa Ana winds had died down. Most of my neighbors in our tight little community had vowed to stay and defy the mandatory evacuation order the way many of us did after the slide in 2005. It was not that we would not evacuate, but that we wanted to wait and see what would happen as most of us had animals and other concerns. Following the news and maps, we thought we knew where the fire would be popping over the ridge and were waiting for it. My husband and I live at the top of Sunland Avenue, with only one house between us and the mountain of low brush. That house across Vista del Rincon Street belongs to our good friends, the Malone's, who had just built a new deck in their backyard.

My neighbor on the other side of our house was a gentle giant of a man by the name of John Beck, one of the nicest people I have ever known. John was resolute about staying no matter what. Between the Beck house and ours, there is a fire hydrant. John was able to open it and attach his genuine 150-foot fire hose. It was at 2.30 a.m. that all hell broke loose as the fire surprised us; it came at La Conchita from a different direction than expected and faster too. Before I knew it, the fire was in the Malone's

Above: Photo of the Thomas Fire, across the street from the author's house. (*Author's collection*)

Right: John Beck, 2018. (*Bill Malis*)

backyard, so close to their house I could only imagine it already eating up that new deck, and I was actually feeling the heat of the fire. The fire engines began screaming up our block, but they were aiming their hoses on the hill at the fire blazing away. Who was it blasting the Malone house with water as well as our house? John Beck and his hose. We heard later that he also caught the sparks that sailed through the sky like heat -seeking missiles and landed on vulnerable houses on the next block. Some of our other Sunland Avenue neighbors—Tim, Steve, and Filipe—assisted by moving John's massive hose wherever it was needed. Watching John and his hose was the last image I saw as fire fighters helped us into our car, to head off the block and out of La Conchita. I was sure as we rode into Santa Barbara to stay with our friend, Claudia, that despite John's heroic efforts, my house as well as other houses close to the hill were probably all lost.

Having witnessed the determination of that fire when we left, I could not imagine another turnout. The next day, when we learned that everyone's home had been spared (including the Malone's deck), I realized I had witnessed an incredible act of heroism—John had worked on alongside the fire fighters throughout the night to make sure none of his neighbors' houses caught fire. It had been all those massive flares that made the Thomas Fire spread so quickly beyond areas that had burnable material. It enabled that fire to escape any natural containment by sending out shoots to start new fires in new places. In the aftermath of "La Conchita's miraculous survival from the Thomas Fire," reading a number of the national media accounts (from NBC News to the *San Francisco Chronicle*) of what happened that early morning in La Conchita is far from what I know to be the case. Everybody wants to take a bow, even people who were not there or did nothing. The articles I read never mention the real hero mostly responsible for saving large sections of La Conchita by name, and the primary source of information in their articles slept through the catastrophe early that morning.

John and the guys on our block are the last people who would seek credit for staying up all night to help save our community ; that is why I love living here. When we arrived back home, everyone knew we "had dodged a bullet." At least, that is what the guys say. The women mostly say, "it was a miracle." The meteorologists say maybe we got a surprise hand from "a strange shift in the wind at just the right time." I say, "every once in a while, David gets a chance to slay Goliath." It reminds us that even in the worst of times; impossible is only a word not a belief or an action.

In Memory of John Beck

A few months after John Beck saved La Conchita from the Thomas Fire, he died of cancer at sixty years old. It stunned us all. John was the essence of La Conchita—quirky, for sure, but also unique, humane, life-loving, eccentrically creative, multi-focused, and unafraid to be different. Just thinking about John now saving the community with that official fire hose is making me laugh rather than cry. What did I tell you about La Conchita's obsessive collectors? How many other people could have just whipped out a 150-foot official fire hose, the kind firemen use to attach to hydrants, and put out fires from their collection of stuff in the garage? He embodied these qualities as well as being generous and kind. John was also a great storyteller. My favorite John story was about Bill, his pet goat. Everyone was pressuring him to get rid of the goat because its long sharp horns were capable of dissecting someone. John solved the problem by impaling tennis balls at the end of each horn; these became part of the goat's permanent attire.

Seeing his imposing 6-foot 5-inch presence with long ponytail, bare -chested no matter what the weather, with his two big mastiffs, Kilo and Milo walking towards the beach, was part of life on Sunland Avenue. John would always greet me by telling me not to be afraid of "the puppies," and I would say, "then how come they are growling and baring their teeth at me like I'm breakfast?" He would laugh. John had a great laugh. He would say, "you know, the dogs and I love having these conversations with you, we think you're very funny. That's why they're growling. You're the only one left in La Conchita who doesn't know what big wimps these two puppies are. They are supposed to be big bad dogs; you're the only one that lets them pretend to be that." When I looked at those big slobbering creatures, I could swear they were laughing at me.

A week or so after the triumph over the Thomas Fire, we had John and his wife, Janell, over for dinner. He gave us two soft-covered small press poetry books by a fascinating writer he was really into named James Ph. Kotsybar. This philosopher poet writes primarily in a speculative mode about science, time, all forms of life, nature, and outer space. John and I spent part of the evening discussing Kotsybar's writings. It is funny as despite knowing John all of these years, this was not something I would have guessed interested him. He was certainly a multi-faceted person, full of surprises. La Conchita will not be the same without him. Walking down to the beach this past Monday and passing the Beck house, I stopped and closed my eyes for a moment. In my mind's eye, I could see him and heard him greet me as he usually did by telling me not to be afraid of "the puppies." He always loved hearing my reply: "What puppies? All I see are two mountain lions crossed with grizzly bears." He would really laugh. Then he would say, "These puppies are as mild mannered as guppies." My reply was "Right, aren't those the fish that eat their young?" Then, we would both really laugh; even the dogs thought it was funny. Ah, John, you will be greatly missed by us all.

Enraptured by the infinite night sky
That beckons, like a seductive teacher,
inciting me to ask the questions why,
I find no need for pulpit or preacher.
Divinity quietly winks at me
with billions of twinkling eyes until
I'm drawn into majestic mystery,
enticed to understand this thrill,
I am myself the dust of what I view[1]

PHYLLIS BECK: AN ANGEL INCOGNITO

My dear departed friend Phyllis made me believe in fairy godmothers. One thing is perfectly clear to me: if I had not been living in La Conchita with my friend Phyllis watching over me, I would be dead.

She was this fragile, delicate-looking creature with a very kind face who took care of neighbor's pets while they were gone, rode a recumbent three-wheeled bike around town, had a beautiful garden, and would always offer to help you with yours. She was Roger Brown's hospice nurse, but being a very ethical person, she did not want to discuss much with me. They did talk about his garden and his ceramics, and she was delighted to find out he went to flea markets and those types of places. Hearing all about out-of-the-way places made him very happy. Phyllis and I became fast friends. I took her to the art museum and art galleries, which scared her to death, though I never understood why.

People are scared of art. I told her if I could get over being scared of those monster dogs her step son had, she could get over being scared of art. When I had abdominal surgery, and the suture became infected due to a problem at the hospital, Phyllis stepped in and offered to come over every day to take care of the infection. Why is she an angel and how does this relate to something magical happening in La Conchita? Phyllis was retired for ten years, living next door to us in a postage-stamp sized place. Within a year of each other, my husband and I both developed deadly, very aggressive cancers and were late in having them properly diagnosed. We could not get in to see a doctor either in Ventura or Santa Barbara that could help us before it would be too late. In my case, my rheumatologist (I have lupus) had phoned a number of affiliated oncologists in Santa Barbara, who could not totally recognize my cancer but seeing it was fourth stage passed on taking me on. In my husband's case, his emergency happened almost a year before mine and was quasi-diagnosed as a rapidly growing squamous carcinoma by two physicians who were on a tour in Provence with us.

When we got home, Bill called our delightful primary care physician, who told him he could have an appointment in two weeks. Phyllis, of course, who saw this thing growing on Bill's face so fast I was getting ready to give it a name, just said that would not do. Within the next few days, we were in the office of dermatologist Dr. Patricia Walker, only 3.5 miles from our house in Carpinteria. She was someone Phyllis knew. After the examination, Dr. Walker removed the whole cancer with the biopsy—what serendipity. Dr. Walker's husband just happened to be a Mohs cancer surgeon, who primarily worked in San Francisco. Two weeks later, he came down to his wife's office with his surgical team to finish the job on my husband and cosmetically close up. Bill was as good as new.

I was Phyllis's next calamity. I had been limping around for about two weeks and just thinking that I had strained my leg with over exercise. By the time I got to my rheumatologist, however, it was clear there was something really wrong. Whatever it was, it was strange enough for the lab aids to lose their masks of composure for a minute or two. The MRI revealed that the bone marrow in my femur had been replaced by tumors that were getting so big they were causing deformity in that heavy bone. This cancer had metastasized through my bones and changed its form as it traveled through my body and into my lymph nodes, aggressively taking over at an alarming pace.

Somebody said I was a dead duck, though it was not me. My rheumatologist, Dr. Burks—who is really the one who knew there was something wrong and ordered the first MRI and then the PET scan—had called all over to oncologists in Santa Barbara, trying to get someone to see me to no avail. She felt miserable when she called me. My primary care physician is in Ventura. Health care between counties here in California is a challenge, and trying to get your medical records to your doctor in the next county without hand-carrying it is like trying to sneak an illegal immigrant across the border.

When I got home, I just started to cry. Phyllis checked in to see how it went with my doctor, and in between sobs, I relayed my story. Ever the resourceful optimist, she said, "we aren't giving up, let me make a phone call." The next thing I knew, Phyllis and I were in the oncology center at the Ventura County Medical Center (which Santa Barbara considers to be second class to its own medical facilities). Phyllis introduced me to Dr. Slater, who looked at my scans and said, "You know I may know the only doctor who knows what this is." A few minutes later, my hero walked into the room and asked if I had an autoimmune disease. This was Dr. John Prichard, a hematologist and the man ultimately, against the odds, who saved my life with a very aggressive treatment, through two years of hell; I have all the permanent side effects of the treatments to prove it, but I am still here and I could not have a more caring doctor. Who was it that knew where this invisible path to my life saver was? Once again, it was my sweet modest little neighbor Phyllis—our protector and angel incognito; every community should have one. We learned after Phyllis passed away that other people had similar amazing Phyllis stories.

After the medical community in two counties failed us both, this sweet, unassuming woman approaching her eightieth year quietly and miraculously knew exactly where to go, and everyone opened the doors for her so she could save both our lives seven years ago. I have never known anyone else like this, so I am just going to say it—only in La Conchita.

Phyllis Beck, date unknown.
(*Author's collection*)

13

EPILOGUE: MARINE MAMMAL SOUP AND MONARCH MAGIC

Why do I love it here? There are those people I know who will never open their eyes, and they joke that my husband and I have always loved living in "slightly seedy" places. They miss the point, as do other people who are uncomfortable with earnest conversation or have yet to clear their minds and walked a couple of blocks and down to the beach in La Conchita.

I look at this place and what I see is "emergence." Both people and a place in the process of "becoming;" to me, there is nothing more exciting than that. People pass by and overlook this little place and some of the most amazing people; creative innovation and a zest for life have come out of it, from what was very probably the first integrated public school in all of California, to a banana plantation that grew varieties of the fruit that horticulturists insisted could never grow anywhere in California. It continues to attract and inspire some very creative talents. One of the miracles of La Conchita is its unique microclimate; everything grows here. If you have a dying house plant, take it outside and stick it in La Conchita's soil. Let it receive the nightly ocean mist, the rich soil, and whatever magic comes from the mountain. Your dying plant will very likely turn into a tree.

Whenever I think of La Conchita's microclimate, I automatically think of the late Harold Carver, who built one of the first large houses at the base of mountain on the aptly named street Vista del Rincon. Carver was a spritely gentleman in his mid-eighties and lived just up the street from us. My husband and I both patiently listened to the many retellings of Harold's exploits as a World War II bomber pilot. Upon retirement, without the aid of the internet, he undertook world research to find the most temperate place to retire. Somehow, he found La Conchita and read about its near-tropical microclimate without the heat, humidity, or bugs; that is why he decided to spend the rest of his life here with his late wife, Alice. He became a passionate gardener and purchased a parcel of property directly across the street from us, which was a marvel of various fruit trees and other edible veggies. When we crossed paths with him, he loved to regale us with his

Dolphin signs. (*Author's collection*)

Monarch in Chrysalis. (*Author's collection*)

Monarch emerging from Chrysalis. (*Author's collection*)

war stories. The most impressive tale was his crossing the English Channel on fumes and sputtering to a safe landing after passing over the white cliffs of Dover. The avocado tree he planted in the 1950s is now monumental in size and continues to provide residents with fallen fruit. Although he was not among the early pioneers of this little paradise, Harold Carver certainly was a fitting member of La Conchita's cast of characters.

Fertile with energy everywhere, both in nature and people, in La Conchita's Rincon Bay, there is more. La Conchita may have lost the abundant shellfish the Elders reminisced about. We cannot wade out, stick our hands in the sand, and come out holding lobsters anymore, but our waters have what locals fondly call "Marine Mammal Soup" in the bay. The waters are richly populated by the playful creatures that seem to make all humans happy. People long to see them in the wild on vacation. There is just something about seeing them that makes people feel closer to the gentle side of nature when close to creatures that like human beings. They are curious, friendly, and fun to watch. A bountiful number of them live or pass through our area of Rincon Bay, which has been part of a vast, federally protected Marine Mammal Sanctuary since 1980. Just a five-minute drive north and right over the border into Santa Barbara County (roughly 3 miles) is the birthing place for a colony of over 200 harbor seals. They have been giving birth to their babies on a beach with a natural cove for as far back as local historians have recorded; this takes place between January and May every year. The way the beach is situated, visitors can witness the births and mothers nursing and playing with their pups from an overlook above without disturbing them. Volunteer seal watchers are on duty every day at the overlook, counting the births, waving off trespassers, and calling an emergency if there is a threat to the colony on the beach. Seals and their pups are common visitors to our part of Rincon Bay.

Dolphins are also regularly seen doing their choreographed leaps, generally in early morning or late afternoon. They do particularly enjoy playing with the surfers and every once in a while, they cannot resist showing off by accompanying the winning surfers during the Rincon Classic Surfing Competition. A number of years ago, during a very competitive classic, four or five dolphins beat the competing surfers almost all the way to shore. So many people caught this amazing moment on their cameras and cell phones that it was broadcast on Wide World of Sports and picked up by almost all of the major news outlets.

The great metaphor for La Conchita's emergence is that it is on the annual trail of the Monarch Butterfly migration. This little hip pocket of paradise on the Gold Coast hosts hundreds of them every year, where they lay their eggs. We all do our part, ready with the special butterfly plants—the only ones the caterpillars will eat—and then we watch as the undulating dervishes magically transform themselves into the most amazing green jewel of a chrysalis. We wait, watch, and protect as expectant grandparents hoping to catch a glimpse of the miraculous emergence of the Monarch from its green-jeweled prison. We hover, moving it away from predators until its wings dry and it has a fair chance to fly away and survive. Like the Monarch, La Conchita has had a magnificent story of emergence, amazing transformations, and survival.

ENDNOTES

Chapter 1

1. Barre, R., *The Innocents* (Walker: New York, 1995), p. 4.

Chapter 3

1. Richardson, P., interview with author, January 14, 2006.
2. Gallardo, E., interview with author, September 2, 2006.
3. Talaugon, Jr., F., interview with author by telephone, June 2010.

Chapter 5

1. Dacayana, C., email interview with author, September 27, 2009.

Chapter 6

1. McDonough, M. G., interview with author, July 12, 2008.

Chapter 11

1. Lowe, N., p. 27, 6/2010, *Roger Brown: Calif. U.S.A.* 2010, SAIC.

Chapter 12

1. Kotsybar, J. P., "Nobody Ever Told Me This in Science Classroom."

Bibliography

"A Battle to Preserve Solitude," *Ventura Star*, December 4, 1983

"Firm to Settle Suit of Fatat LC Slide," *Los Angeles Times*, September 9, 2008

"La Conchita has its day in the sun," *Coastal View News*, November 18, 2010

"La Conchita Prime Development Area," *Ocean View Properties Brochure*

"Landslide Kills 4 Buried Mountain Deep," January 24, 1909

"LC Residents Can't see Beach," *Ventura Star*, *c*. 1971

"New Photographic History Book," Carpinteria Valley History Society, September/October 2009

"New volume added to History Library," *Coastal View News*, August 27, 2009

"New Well near La Conchita," *Ventura Free Press*, June 28, 1928

"Proposed Rincon Highway Route," December 28, 1969

"Ranch Blamed in Slide Selling Assets," *Santa Barbara News Press*, September 2008

"Rincon Seawall Washout," *California Highway Bulletin*, April 14, 1925

"Roger Brown: Calif., USA," School of the Art Institute of Chicago, 2010

"Success comes in Bunches," *People Weekly*, August 8, 1988

"US Highway 101—1912 to 1959," California Highways, March–April 1960

"Ventura Freeway 101 Dedication," Ventura County Development Association, December 21, 1972

Barre, R., *The Innocents* (Walker Publishing Co.: NY, 1995)

Bates, E., *Rincon del Mar Ranch 1920–1940*, unpublished diary, 27 April 1979

Bentley, A., *Slide, now lawsuits plague La Conchita*

Blow, B., "Rincon Causeway," *California Highway Bulletin*, 1920; "Highway Battles with Sea," *National Motorist*, October 1934; "The King's Highway—Modern Version," *National Motorist*, April 1934

Bortnick., B., "Banana Grower Splits," *Santa Barbara News Press*, February 8, 1998

Boyd, L., "Bates Beauty prepares to leave Ranch," *Coastal View News*, November 23, 1917

Braningham, B, "Pride Without Prejudice," *Santa Barbara Independent*, February 24, 2011; "1909 Slide at LC Claims Lives," *Santa Barbara News Press*

Brown, E. B.,"La Conchita: Where We Live and Why," *Ventura Star*, June 28, 1972

Burns, M., "Megaslide Menace," *Santa Barbara News Press*, October 20, 2005

Campos, J., Kelm, B, Moore D., and T., *Images of America: Greater Carpinteria, Summerland, and La Conchita* (Arcadia Publishing, 2009)

Chase, J. S., *California Coast Trails* (Houghton Mifflin Co.)
Colin Marshall, C., "Latest books from Locals," *The Independent*, October 1, 2009
Cortelyou, S., "Coast Highway," *California Highways*, September–October 1949
Crowder, J., "Close to Home," *Santa Barbara News Press*, November 29, 1996
Dickey, G., "Riprap Job, Engineers Fight Ocean," *California Highways*, January–February 1955
Hernandez, R., "La Conchita Plaintiffs to Get Ranch," *Ventura Star*, September 9, 2008; "La Conchita Ranch sold for $2.5 Million," *Ventura Star*, November 22, 2008
Hollenhorst, L., "Growin' Bananas," *Organic Gardening*, September 1989
Johnson, B., "Round two of LC case kicks off," *Ventura Star*, November 18, 1998; "US Reviews Debris Removal Plans," *Ventura Star*, January 24, 1999
Kilburn, J., "Fifty Years Together as One," *Port Orford News*, July 8, 2001
Kisken, T., "Decade Review: La Conchita Landslide," *Ventura Star*, December 31, 2009
McCurry, "Rincon Causeway," *California Highway Bulletin*
McLain, J., "Foster Parents ... Dacayanas," *Ventura Star*, January 8, 1978
Miller, D., "Ventura Seawall Survives Temblor," *California Highway Bulletin*, August 1925
Noone, D., "Rincon Dwellers Upset by Ocean Gift," *Ventura Star*, September 25, 1982
Pascual., P., "A Banana Bonanza," *Los Angeles Times*, July 9, 1990
Redmon, M., "Santa Barbara and Ventura Counties, Once One," *The Independent*, December 8, 2005
Reynolds, C., "The Town at the End of the Tunnel," *Los Angeles Times*, August 22, 1991
Rouse, S. H., "Rincon's Little Volcano," *Santa Barbara News Press*, November 28, 1965
Saillant, C., "Firm to Settle Suit Over Slide," *Los Angeles Times*, September 9, 2008; "US Reviews plans for debris at LC," January 24, 1999
Scott Wilson, S., "La Conchita, Ragged Past, Rocky Future," *Santa Barbara News Press*, March 19, 1995
Smalley, J., "Rincon Pioneer Families," *Ventura Star*, January 8, 1967
Smith, W., "Cheap homesites in La Conchita," *Ventura Star*, n.d.
Steve Chawkins, S., "Caltrans Decked La Conchita Deck," *Ventura Star*, March 23, 1997
Wagner., D. "County has its own Volcano," *Vista*, August 15, 1985
Warchol., R., "Legal Dispute over Bates Ranch," *Los Angeles Times*, December 18, 1994
"Wife Sues Warner Oland for Divorce," *Los Angeles Times*, August 12, 1937
Wood, C., "America's Camino Real," *Concrete Highways and Improvements*, July 1928

Oral Histories

Blackwell, A., interview with author and documents.
Blackwell, R., emails, phone interview with author, documents and photos.
Dacayana, B., interview with author and materials, December 2, 2007–September 10, 2008.
Dacayana, C., numerous interviews through phone calls and emails plus documents.
Gallardo, E., interview with author and materials, December 8, 2005.
Hutto, R., interview with author and materials, February 5, 2007.
McDonough, M. J. (Giles), interview with author and materials, December 15, 2008.
Mingus, B., email and phone interviews, notes and documents, 1954 photo book.
Richardson, P., interview with author, January 14, 2006.
Talaugon, D., interview with author, December 18, 2005.
Talaugon-Dunn, B., interview with author and documents, October 6, 2008.